*Start*Book

Launching New Entrepreneurs

Evan Keller

with Odile Pérez, Carson Weitnauer & Jeff Hostetter

*Creating*Jobs**.org**
Business for Global Good

Creating Jobs Inc
DeLand, Florida

Published by:

Creating Jobs Inc
136 S. Sheridan Ave.
DeLand FL 32720
World Wide Web: www.creatingjobs.org
E-mail: info@creatingjobs.org
ISBN 978-0-9967216-7-7

Printed in the United States of America

Dedication

Were you ever instantly inspired by someone who has surmounted huge obstacles by the grace of God? The idea for this book was born in Honduras the week we met Joyce, a 17-year-old who supports a household of eight and three employees through her hair salon. That day in August 2017, we were amazed that she'd launched a successful business while attending college and parenting her three younger brothers.

It's amazing to see first-hand how Compassion International shapes the character and leadership of countless young lives. We are overjoyed to work with them to help other teens in Honduras and around the world to do what Joyce has done.

Thank you Joyce for inspiring us and your fellow teens to help communities thrive!

Table of Contents

1

*Start*Book

Snapshot:

Mobilize your strengths, resources and teammates to bring an innovative solution to customers who want it.

StartBook

At-a-Glance

Mobilize your strengths, resources and teammates to bring an innovative solution to customers who want it.

1. You

Learn what makes a mature entrepreneur. Assess yourself and plan to grow.

2. Solution

Create a unique solution to a real problem, letting your customers' input shape your product or service. Build your business identity around that solution and design systems to produce your product efficiently and safely.

3. People

Appreciate and learn from these groups of people who are vital to your success. Build trusting win-win relationships with them.

4. Money

There's never enough money for everything, so you must direct it toward your priorities. Diligently follow these best practices to control your money and patiently build wealth.

5. Launch

Give attention to these important details to plan a successful launch.

6. Customers

Identify your ideal customers and find the right message and means to reach them. Make them so happy that they bring their friends to you.

7. Growth

Plan your next steps to put StartBook into practice. Decide whether you want to grow from a solopreneur into a CEO of a strong company.

11

What does each aspect of your business need?
Write "maintain", "fine-tune", or "overhaul" under each icon.

My *BiG* Focus:

My top goal to
move it forward:

Introduction

For our teen readers, we hope and pray that this book will be the start of an amazing journey that transforms you as you create a business that helps your community thrive. If you focus on growing your character as we suggest here, and work both smart and hard, you will be amazed at what God will do through you.

This is not a complicated textbook filled with fancy words. No. *Start*Book breaks the complexities of business down into super simple action steps that you can definitely do if you remain determined – for several years! There are tons of things that can be done in business, but some are more effective than others. This book gives you the bare essentials. No fluff here. Only actions that bring results. (To drive this point home, each lesson is an action and we've italicized the main verbs in the headings throughout *Start*Book.)

Business really *can* be made simple, but that doesn't mean it's easy. Making a business succeed is one of the hardest and most rewarding things you'll ever attempt. And creating something this valuable to your community is a great way to imitate your Creator. He will give you the creativity, strength and wisdom as you trust in Him. But you must take *action*, pouring steady initiative into doing the right things over and over. This book isn't theory – it is a roadmap that we've already travelled as we've built our own successful businesses. Follow the advice and examples of the entrepreneurs on these pages and this map will work for you too. Take courage – you can do this!

Here's a quick word on how to use the tools in this book. Notice the "Big Picture" at the beginning and end of the book. It is a quick self-assessment that should only take a couple of minutes to fill out. You can use it to measure your progress by taking it before and after you apply our advice.

After each of the seven modules is another tool called "*Start*Book Plan". As you finish each module, please use this tool to set goals to apply what you've learned. There is a vast difference between knowing something intellectually versus by experience. You quickly forget other people's ideas, but if you try them out, they become part of you and can change you dramatically for the better. Module 7 shares more about how to use the *Start*Book Plan, which is found again at the end of the book.

Throughout *Start*Book, we provide exercises to help you start small in applying these ideas at home, school, and church. Using these can make what you're learning a part of your life, but the best learning will happen when you apply our advice to an actual business that you start.

Reflecting is almost as important as acting, so this book is filled with Scriptures and questions to get you thinking about how to grow yourself and your business. There are places to write down your reflections which can lead you back into action. We encourage you not to skip this important step as writing is a powerful way to focus and capture your thoughts for future use.

You'll see that the lessons are chockful of expert advice to follow. To show you how they're applied in real life, we give you case studies of how actual businesses have put our advice into practice. Each module also has a fictional narrative of a pair of teens who are wrestling with how to start a successful business.

We pray and believe that you can: create jobs for people who need them, produce products and services that meet real needs, provide well for your own family, and become a strong leader in your church and community – all to the glory of God!

1. You

Module snapshot: Learn what makes a mature entrepreneur. Assess yourself and plan to grow.

Module 1: YOU

 Consider module snapshot: Learn what makes a mature entrepreneur. Assess yourself and plan to grow.

 Observe teens who need advice:

One Sunday at Grace Fellowship Church, Mario, a seventeen-year old, stood up to tell his story of coming to know Jesus. It was an amazing story of God's miraculous intervention in his life. At the end, the pastor asked Mario how the church could pray for him. Unexpectedly, Mario's face turned from joyful to anxious, as he shared the struggles he faced in finding a job and feeding his younger sisters.

As regular church members at Grace Fellowship, Alejandro and Maria — two best friends — were listening carefully. As they left the church, Alejandro said to Maria, "I think God gave me a vision while Mario was speaking. I think we're supposed to start a tortilleria – and hire Mario."

Alejandro was a bold risk-taker always on the go. Maria preferred to take her time in coming to a decision. So, as usual, she paused and thought for a moment. Then she said, "But Alejandro, we don't know *anything* about business! So if this is true, then God will have to show us what to do. We know God loves us as His own children! Let's pray and ask the Holy Spirit to guide us!"

Alejandro responded, "That's a good idea, Maria, but let's start right away - over lunch! I want to go to Tortilleria Carolina and get some ideas for our business."

Lesson 1A: *Find* your identity in Christ

 Follow expert advice (*Find* your identity in Christ):

Knowing that you are completely accepted and lavishly loved by God is the only true anchor in the rough seas of life. As a royal son or daughter of God, you have ample confidence and courage to do anything He calls you to do. Your value is demonstrated by Christ's sacrifice for you rather than by anything you accomplish. So you are free to take great risks without cutting corners or mistreating others. And whether you experience success or failure, God will use it to make you more like Jesus.

Knowing who you are allows you to build your life on the rock. This conquers fear, anxiety, indecision, and settling for less than your full potential. If God's purpose for you on earth is unfinished, you are indestructible. If the ultimate enemy, death, cannot interrupt God's call on your life, then why worry about the small stuff? Not only does God give you the breath of life, but he's stamped His own creative image on you and given the responsibility to develop the potential of His good creation. For example, think about the windmills on the mountains south of Tegucigalpa, Honduras. In His gift of creation, God provided many gifts that culminated in those wind turbines. Can you list a few? Wind, the idea to harness it and turn it into power, electricity itself, iron ore, silicon and other minerals. God also gives *you* the gifts you need to do what he's called you to do. Since he wanted to provide wind-generated power to Tegucigalpa, he gifted people over many centuries to turn iron into steel, petroleum into plastic, and silicon into computer chips.

Obeying God's call to use His gifts in us and around you brings lots of joy. It's the joy of co-creating with God, in gratitude for His gifts, the satisfaction of using your mind and body to bring something new into the world that serves your community. It's joyful because in it you are fulfilling God's call to love your neighbors. You have all the freedom to explore creating out of God's gifts without the pressure of getting it wrong. As you learn what you are good at and how to use it to love your neighbor, you will make mistakes along the way. It's called failure. The cool thing is that your mistakes don't in the least bit diminish who you are: a lavishly loved child of God. You can pour your whole heart into everything you do knowing that if you fall flat on your face, you are still someone for whom Christ willingly died to save! Like a dad who teaches his daughter to ride a bike, he wants her to grow in courage and experience the joy of a new and faster way to travel. If she falls, he picks her up with compassion and helps her try again. She's no less his daughter after falling and his belief in her instills confidence. You have infinite value as God's beloved and have His gifts and empowerment to follow Jesus in humbly serving others.

So depend on God, use your gifts, and give your all without fear. Learn to receive God's relentless affection for you and you'll be unstoppable. "Perfect love drives out fear" (1 John 4:18, HCSB).

 Ask yourself (*Find* your identity in Christ):

Do I find my core identity in what I've done or in what Christ has done for me?

_____

How can I draw strength from God's love when I'm tempted to be fearful?

_____

What talents has God given me?

_____

_____

Knowing that my failures cannot diminish who I am as God's child, what risk can I confidently take to put those talents to use?

_____

_____

 Meditate on these scriptures (*Find* your identity in Christ):

Love creates security. 1 John 4:18 (NLT): *"Such love has no fear, because perfect love expels all fear."*

The security of being God's child reminds you that risking failure doesn't jeopardize what is most important. Romans 8:14-19 (ESV): *"For all who are led by the Spirit of God are sons of God. For you did not receive the spirit of slavery to fall back into fear, but you have received the Spirit of adoption as sons, by whom we cry, 'Abba! Father!' The Spirit himself bears witness with our spirit that we are children of God, and if children, then heirs—heirs of God and fellow heirs with Christ, provided we suffer with him in order that we may also be glorified with him. For I consider that the sufferings of this present time are not worth comparing with the glory that is to be revealed to us. For the creation waits with eager longing for the revealing of the sons of God."*

Confidence in God's call gives you courage in trials. Nehemiah 6 (ESV): When Sanballat threatened Nehemiah's life to derail his rebuilding of Jerusalem's wall, he replied: *"I am doing a great work"*, *"I cannot [be distracted]"*, *I will not [hide to save my life]"*. Instead, he prayed: *"But now, O God, strengthen my hands."* When he completed *the wall, Israel's enemies "recognized that this work had been accomplished with the help of our God."*

Lesson 1B: *Gain* the biblical mindset on business and money:

 Follow expert advice (*Gain* the biblical mindset on business and money):

Work is an honorable way to imitate God and his creativity. Business is God's way of answering the Lord's Prayer for daily bread (Matthew 6:11). Even money is a tool that can accomplish much good.

Work is good because God works. When God created the world, he rejoiced that it was "very good". The bible offers many metaphors of God as a worker. He's pictured as a: "potter, metalworker, garment maker, dresser, gardener, farmer, winemaker, shepherd, tentmaker, builder, architect, musician, and composer....He inspires and equips all good work." (Witherington, p.7) As part of reflecting his image, you are the only creatures to whom he entrusted the privilege of joining him as a worker. Work is a good gift, beginning with Adam being charged with naming the animals, tending the garden, and being put in charge of the whole earth! When Adam and Eve disobeyed God, your work was corrupted with toil and frustration, but still retains goodness that can be deeply fulfilling.

Business is a way of organizing work to optimize the value (products) it creates for people (customers). Obeying God's call to develop His creation, business creatively combines raw materials with innovation and work to meet the real needs people have. So, business is a good thing because it combines good ingredients: God's good creation, creative minds which reflect their Creator, and human bodies doing good work. This recipe comes together to serve up products and services that help communities thrive around the world. The money your business makes (sales minus expenses) is called "profit". Profit is not evil as some claim, but rather measures how much value you've created for people in your community.

Money is a good thing. Imagine how hard it would be if people couldn't convert the results of their work into something that everyone wanted. It would make everything so much harder if the farmer tried to buy medicine, education, and gasoline with potatoes! Like any good gift, money can be distorted into a dangerous idol. It is a tool that can be used for evil but also for incredible good in service to others.

Embracing God's perspective on work, business, and money will prepare you to become a successful entrepreneur. And it gives you a part in showing how Jesus is Lord over business as well as every part of life and society. Enjoy the awesome privilege of being a co-worker with the Almighty!

Ask yourself (*Gain* the biblical mindset on business and money):

How does God's work change my view of my work?

_____

_____

Which benefits of business excite me?

_____

_____

How does this challenge my view of money?

_____

_____

What have I experienced of the struggle between greed and generosity?

_____

_____

Meditate on these scriptures (*Gain* the biblical mindset on business and money):

Work is good because God is the original worker. Genesis 1:31 (NIV): "God saw all that He had made, and it was very good. And there was evening, and there was morning—the sixth day."

Work is a significant part of God's purpose for humanity. Genesis 2:15 (NIV): "The LORD God took the man and put him in the Garden of Eden to work it and take care of it."

Wealth creation is a gift from God. Deuteronomy 8:18 (NIV): *"But remember the LORD your God, for it is He who gives you the ability to produce wealth."*

Money in the right hands can significantly bless a community. Proverbs 11:10-11 (NIV): *"When the righteous prosper, the city rejoices; when the wicked perish, there are shouts of joy. Through the blessing of the upright a city is exalted, but by the mouth of the wicked it is destroyed."*

God uses business to answer prayer. Matthew 6:11 (NIV): *"Give us today our daily bread."*

Lesson 1C: *Grow* in Character

 Follow expert advice (*Grow* in character):

Entrepreneurs are: determined, creative, problem-solvers, optimistic, courageous in facing risks, future focused, self-controlled, hard workers, continual learners, humble, servant-hearted, action-oriented, trustworthy, and full of integrity. Discover which of the above character traits you are strong and weak in, then ask God to help you build habits that reshape your character over time.

As the only human with perfect character, Jesus models how God wants us to live. In fact, making us like Jesus is God's primary will for our lives. That's it! Romans 8:29 says our destiny is to be "conformed to the image of his son." We all want to be like Jesus...in theory! But when we take a closer look, we notice that Jesus lived a cross-shaped life (Hood, 2013, p.67). You are made like Jesus as you obey his command to "deny yourself, take up your cross and follow me." You grow in character as you imitate Jesus' self-sacrificing love. You are incapable of living like Jesus without God empowering you, so constantly ask for him to shape you by his Spirit. As you surrender to this "dying to yourself" over and over and over, it becomes a habit. If you're seeking to be more honest, the twentieth time you resist telling a lie should be a little easier than the first time. Several things are happening to you, including: sensing God's pleasure, enjoying more authentic relationships, and building a new habit with accompanying neural pathways in your brain. Over time, habits harden into traits – they become part of who you are (Kahle, Businessasmission.com).

But what does character have to do with business? The success of a business relies heavily on the character of its leader. This is true because your business will take on your personality, and customers strongly desire to do business with people they trust. In addition to Christ-like character, there are general personality traits that combine to make great entrepreneurs. These are the traits you'll need the most to succeed in business:

Determined – This is the *most necessary* trait because starting a business requires doing hard things for many hours every day over a period of years with no guarantee of success and no one pushing you to do them. The fire must come from within. It must burn long and hard. It involves weathering many small failures while believing ultimate success is certain.

Creative – You must dream up innovative solutions for customers, and build them into amazing products and services. Then you've got to relish the challenge of making your business better every day. Always think up new ideas for every part of your business, write them down, and try them out.

Problem-solvers – Things will go wrong *every day* in your business, so you'll need to be decisive in solving problems. Rather than reacting with fear or anger or paralysis, you must learn to coolly and humbly face adversity head-on. Sometimes the problems will seem insurmountable, yet you'll need to rise to the challenge day after day after day. Many of the problems will be caused by people who cheat you. In fact, you'll be amazed at the variety of scams and thefts that your business will attract. Business will "thicken your skin" (increase your tolerance for stress). As you grow in wisdom and experience, your decisions will improve and bad people won't rob you of sleep.

"Another important aspect of being a problem solver in business is to meet a real need instead of just providing something people can easily live without. When you solve a real problem and meet a true need, people's lives become better and they appreciate that. This is a powerful way for you to imitate God himself! He is the ultimate problem solver." (Jeff Hostetter) Our sin problem damaged our relationships with God, his Creation, and each other. Instead of giving up on his rebellious humans, He patiently began a series of provisional solutions that culminated in the sacrifice of his son Jesus on the cross. Those solutions included creating a people that belong to him, then sending them a deliverer and law-giver (Moses), judges, priests, prophets, and kings, and inspiring the biblical writers to reveal the way back to God. By sending his Son, he personally entered our problems, and through his death and resurrection broke the chokehold that sin and death had on us. While you cannot free people from their sins, there is a way you can imitate the ultimate problem-solver. When Jesus provided healing, freed people from demons, fed and touched and spoke healing words to them, he established the importance of alleviating all types of human need, including our physical, emotional, spiritual, and social ones. So when entrepreneurs solve problems for people, they can be the hands and feet of Jesus. What an amazing privilege!

Optimistic – Despite the constant battles, you must believe you'll win the war. Cheerfulness and humor can ease your stress. Optimism's best foundation is finding your identity in Christ and knowing that your business is part of God's plan to reveal his glory in your community. In contrast, believing the worst case scenario can cripple your motivation to build a strong business.

Courageous in facing risks – Risk-averse people will not put lots of their time and money on the line when 75% of businesses fail within five years. Analysis and planning are good, but you must know when to step out and act. Courage is not the lack of fear, but taking positive action in the face of fear.

Action-oriented – Entrepreneurs are more likely to be seen acting rather than–merely talking. They get things done; they make things happen. They're not afraid to try out ideas before they are 100% perfected, and they learn more by doing than by planning. They seize opportunities before they slip away.

Future focused – Entrepreneurs are not content with just surviving today. They see what they want to achieve in the future and they make sacrifices today and every day to reach that far off goal. This "delayed gratification" is necessary because building a strong business isn't quick or easy. You must believe you can truly shape your own future with God's help. A strong business can provide a thriving future for entire communities.

Self-controlled – Being disciplined, especially with your time, money, and words will provide stability to your business. But if you are cavalier and loose with how you use your time, money and words, you will sabotage your business. Poor use of time will waste your potential, selfish or wasteful use of money will make you bankrupt, and angry or careless use of words will drive away your employees and customers.

Hard workers – It's impossible to realize how much work a business will be until you actually do it. Eighteen hour days for several years is not unusual. Another surprise is the number of very different kinds of tasks a new entrepreneur needs to do. Recent brain research shows that shifting between tasks and having so many things on your mind at once are very taxing on the brain.

Being constantly interrupted with another urgent matter is an all-day experience for most new entrepreneurs. So, challenges include: prioritizing and organizing the work with your mind, completing the actual work, and training others so you can pass on some of your many "hats" to reliable employees.

Continual learners – Many entrepreneurs have a conflicted relationship with learning. Having accomplished the Herculean task of starting a business, they're tempted to think they don't need to keep learning. No one knows their business better than them, so pride closes their mind from learning – especially from people they consider less accomplished than themselves. On the other hand, the best entrepreneurs know that they need to keep learning to get (or stay) ahead of their competitors. Learning from a variety of people, books, articles, and videos stimulates your creativity. Writing down and acting on new knowledge solidifies what you're learning. Even in his eighties, Warren Buffett reads for 5-6 hours a day! At his age and level of accomplishment – he's the second wealthiest person on earth – he could justifiably say "I think I have it all figured out by now" and just operate from his accumulated wisdom and experience.

Humble – Being able to admit when you're wrong, apologize and make it right can win over disgruntled employees and customers. Humility helps you be open to good ideas from others. Being able to make fun of yourself and relate to your employees on a personal level makes you more approachable and likeable.

Servant-hearted – Since the purpose of business is to serve, customers will sense whether you only want to use them or whether you truly care. Show concern for your employees' families and take an interest in their personal and professional development. Remember, Jesus is our model here.

Trustworthy – "The enduring success of an organization is built on the trustworthiness of its leaders...customers strongly desire to do business with people they trust." (Den Besten, 2008 p.61-62)

Full of integrity – "Business tests people's integrity. How? Integrity is doing what is right – living life God's way. It's living an honest life in which your words and actions match up. Business causes us to face challenging situations and difficult people. Business owners are tempted to cut corners or be dishonest. So we need to be filling our heart and mind with God's principles from scripture and asking the Lord for His strength so it shows up in how we do business, and we maintain our integrity." (Jeff Hostetter)

How well do you embody these traits? Does this list describe you? Because pride can inhibit our self-awareness, don't just trust your own self-reflection! Instead, take assessments (such as StrengthsFinder, Myers-Briggs, and DISC) that can reveal your strengths and personality traits. Also, ask those who know you best to honestly rate you on these character traits. Then choose a few that you need to work on the most and seek God's help in developing new habits through which you can practice them.

Study the life of Jesus. Read biographies of past and present leaders whose example you can follow. Find people in your own community whom you can admire and emulate up close. Growing in character is likely the best investment you can make in both yourself and your business.

Ask yourself (*Grow* in character):

Which of these entrepreneurial character traits am I strong and weak in?

_____

_____

Which mentors and family members can give me an honest assessment of my character?

_____

Which character traits do I most want to have?

_____

How has God used hardships and habits to shape my character?

_____

_____

What habits should I start in order to shape my character over time?

_____

Will I follow Jesus in difficult self-discipline in order to grow more like him?

Am I praying for the Holy Spirit to change me?

 Meditate **on these scriptures (*Grow* in character):**

God's goal for our lives is to make us more like Jesus. Romans 8:29 (ESV): *"For those whom he foreknew he also predestined to be conformed to the image of his Son, in order that he might be the firstborn among many brothers."*

Becoming like Jesus involves reflecting his cross-shaped life. Matthew 16:24 (NIV): *"Whoever wants to be my disciple must deny themselves and take up their cross and follow me."*

Determination is an important virtue. Proverbs 24:16 (NIV): *"For though the righteous fall seven times, they rise again, but the wicked stumble when calamity strikes."*

In God's strength, you can accomplish much more than you now realize. Hebrews 11:32-34 (NIV): *"And what more shall I say? I do not have time to tell about Gideon, Barak, Samson and Jephthah, about David and Samuel and the prophets, who through faith conquered kingdoms, administered justice, and gained what was promised; who shut the mouths of lions, quenched the fury of the* *flames, and escaped the edge of the sword; whose weakness was turned to strength; and who became powerful in battle and routed foreign armies."*

Your customers and employees will sense whether you really care about them or only what you can get from them. Philippians 2:3 (ESV): *"Do nothing from selfish ambition or conceit, but in humility count others more significant than yourselves."*

Being steady when things are hard is necessary in business. James 5:11 (ESV): *"Behold, we consider those blessed who remained steadfast. You have heard of the steadfastness of Job, and you have seen the purpose of the Lord, how the Lord is compassionate and merciful."*

Deal with those who cheat you without being corrupted by them. Matthew 10:16 (NIV): *"I am sending you out like sheep among wolves. Therefore be as shrewd as snakes and as innocent as doves."*

Providing for yourself through diligent work is honorable. 2 Thessalonians 3:8-10 (NIV): *"Nor did we eat anyone's food without paying for it. On the contrary, we worked night and day, laboring and toiling so that we would not be a burden to any of you. We did this, not because we do not have the right to such help, but in order to offer ourselves as a model for you to imitate. For even when we were with you, we gave you this rule: 'The one who is unwilling to work shall not eat.'"*

Honestly assess your abilities before you begin. Romans 12:3 (ESV): *"For by the grace given to me I say to everyone among you not to think of himself more highly than he ought to think, but to think with sober judgment, each according to the measure of faith that God has assigned."*

God is concerned with integrity in your business. Proverbs 16:11 (NIV): *"Honest scales and balances belong to the Lord; all the weights in the bag are of his making."*

Character is the highest form of wealth. Proverbs 28:6 (ESV): *"Better is a poor man who walks in his integrity than a rich man who is crooked in his ways."*

Lesson 1D: *Develop* your business skills

 Follow expert advice (*Develop* your business skills):

Mobilize your talents to meet a need in your community better than anyone else. Before and after launch, find experts and courses to help you develop your skills. As we advised earlier, be a lifelong learner. This will increase your credibility with your customers. Get better every day at your craft and also learn how to build a strong business - which you may find to be the most important skill you need to develop.

It may all start with an opportunity that's in front of you. What can you do with what you have? The biblical prophet Elijah met a widow who was so desperate that she said "Your servant has nothing in the house except a jar of oil (2 Kings 4:2 HCSB)." But Elijah helped her to see and use several *other* things she *already* had, including: God, family, and friends. God blessed and increased what she had as she put them to use. What do *you* have? Like the widow, we often fail to notice what God has given us. We look externally for answers that most of the time already lie within us. Dr. Andrés Panasiuk asserts that "it is not our *abilities* that count for the Creator of the universe, but our *availability* for Him....What matters to Him is that we put them at his *disposal*. That is the determining factor". When we offer our skills to God, He multiplies them and even does miracles with them (Panasiuk, 2015, p.143-148). This is exactly what happened with the widow, and you should follow her example. Focus on your strengths and skills, present them to God, take the necessary actions to put them to use, and trust that He will multiply them!

There's a second widow who illustrates this in our own generation. Dr. Andrés Panasiuk tells a story of a friend named Marta who was widowed as a young mother, left with no way of supporting herself and her son. She didn't know what to do until her uncle offered to help her get training to work in his dental office. She spent time and energy to go to dental school, worked for her uncle, then opened her own practice and grew it into a strong business. Now her son has become a dentist as well! This all came about because adversity forced her to look around for what opportunities God had provided. Like the widow Elijah encountered, this widow was encouraged to see what was already in her hands, and God provided as she put it to use.

Take note at how your skills, hobbies, interests, and passions intersect the needs of the world. That intersection is the perfect recipe for excellent products that are true solutions.

Very few things in life are more fulfilling than the opportunity to every day do what your best at, what you love, what you know God has called you to do! The problem for young people is that they don't always know what they can be great at, and then it takes a long time to grow a potential talent into a world-class talent. In his book Outliers, Malcolm Gladwell says that it takes 10,000 hours of practice to become an expert at something (Gladwell). Another challenge for new entrepreneurs is that what your business most needs from you is not necessary what you love doing the most! You may end up needing to do some less-than-favorite things *for years* until you can hire others who are more gifted in those areas. People usually start a business to sell something they enjoy producing, then they slowly start to realize that rather than making their product, building their business is what they need to focus their time and creative energy on. Yes, creating unique products is important, but world-class products alone doesn't make a business fly. Entrepreneurs need a steady stream of customers and build strong relationships with them. They need to learn to develop employees, master money, plan for growth and provide leadership for every area of the business. To sum it up, the most important skill for an entrepreneur is to see where the business should be heading and provide strategies and plans to take it there. In other words, be a good leader. That's what this book is about: learning to "mobilize your strengths, resources and teammates to bring an innovative solution to customers who want it." This skill you can only learn by doing it. But to start with, your key skill may revolve around making an innovative product that people really want.

Ask yourself (*Develop* your business skills):

What am I good at and really enjoy doing?

_____

_____

"What could I become the best in the world at?" (Jim Collins, 2011, p.13).

_____

_____

How can I more actively develop that skill?

_____

_____

Which of my skills do people seem to value the most?

_____

_____

How do my skills, hobbies, interests, and passions intersect the needs of the world?

_____

_____

What can I do with what I have?

_____

_____

Are there accreditations that I will need to earn my customers' trust? Which experts and courses can help me grow?

_____

_____

Am I better at building my product or building my business and what does my business need more from me right now?

_____

_____

 Meditate on these scriptures (*Develop your business skills*):

Well-developed talents increase influence and access. Proverbs 22:29 (ESV): *"Do you see a man skillful in his work? He will stand before kings; he will not stand before obscure men."*

God gives innate ability and helps you develop it. Exodus 31:1-5 (NIV): *"Then the Lord said to Moses, "See, I have chosen Bezalel son of Uri, the son of Hur, of the tribe of Judah, and I have filled him with the Spirit of God, with wisdom, with understanding, with knowledge* *and with all kinds of skills— to make artistic designs for work in gold, silver and bronze, to cut and set stones, to work in wood, and to engage in all kinds of crafts."*

Honing your talents will accelerate your success. Ecclesiastes 10:10 (ESV): *"If the iron is blunt, and one does not sharpen the edge, he must use more strength, but wisdom helps one to succeed."*

Giving wholehearted effort will develop your potential. Colossians 3:23 (ESV): *"Whatever you do, work at it with all your heart, as working for the Lord, not for human masters."*

God uses what you have to provide your needs and advance his purposes. 1 Kings 17:12-16 (NIV): *"As surely as the LORD your God lives," she replied, "I don't have any bread—only a handful of flour in a jar and a little olive oil in a jug. I am gathering a few sticks to take home and make a meal for myself and my son, that we may eat it— and die." Elijah said to her, "Don't be afraid. Go home and do as you have said. But first make a small loaf of bread for me from what you have and bring it to me, and then make something for yourself and your son. For this is what the LORD, the God of Israel, says: 'The jar of flour will not be used up and the jug of oil will not run dry until the day the LORD sends rain on the land.'" She went away and did as Elijah had told her. So there was food every day for Elijah and for the woman and her family. For the jar of flour was not used up and the jug of oil did not run dry, in keeping with the word of the LORD spoken by Elijah."*

Lesson 1E: *Write* everything down

 Follow expert advice (*Write* everything down):

Writing helps to clarify your thoughts, make them more real, and preserves them for future reflection and action. The sequence of thinking, writing, and acting is essential to creating a strong business.

Twelve years after starting my business, I realize that writing is the most important thing I do. I try to write every day. Here are some of the most important things an entrepreneur writes: company name and tagline, product names, vision, mission, values, goals, plans, systems, policies, marketing messages, and letters to customers or employees or suppliers. Writing is so important because effective communication is a key to good leadership, and writing forces you to communicate clearly and succinctly. So, learn to love words and use them carefully. Don't waste a word; let each one be powerful. Long before Edward Bulwer-Lytton coined the phrase "The pen is mightier than the Sword", God used mere words to speak the universe into existence! Jesus is called the Word since he perfectly reveals God to us. And God inspired people over a long span of time to write the Holy Scriptures. As the best-selling book of all time, the Bible has shaped humanity more than any empire, any king, any army. Even your own words, when they are written down, can be followed for years to come, and be used to shape the thoughts and actions of your employees. Writing is amazing in how it preserves your best ideas to be recalled and built upon later.

So get in the habit of writing *everything* down – ideas you have when you wake up in the morning, notes from reading this and other books, key points from conversations you have with mentors and employees, plans for designing and marketing your products, lists of people and businesses to sell to, policies and systems for your employees to follow, do-lists and schedules, detailed orders from customers, and most importantly: your business vision, mission, values, and goals.

 Ask yourself (*Write* everything down):

Do I love words like God does?

_____

How should I be using this powerful tool?

_____

_____

What are some things I need to take time to write?

_____

_____

Who can help me improve my writing skills?

_____

_____

What parts of my business to I need to think on, write about, then act upon?

_____

_____

 Meditate on these scriptures (*Write* everything down):

Putting things into words helps us do more with them. Genesis 2:19-20 (NIV): *"Now the LORD God had formed out of the ground all the wild animals and all the birds in the sky. He brought them to the man to see what he would name them; and whatever the man called each living creature, that was its name. So the man gave names to all the livestock, the birds in the sky and all the wild animals. But for Adam no suitable helper was found."*

Words are powerful and writing makes them available to many people at many times and in many places. Proverbs 18:21 (ESV): *"Death and life are in the power of the tongue."*

Lesson 1F: *Adapt* business to your life plan:

 Follow expert advice (*Adapt* business to your life plan):

"Your life plan has to come before your business plan" (Brodsky & Burlingham, 2008). This is an important discipline because business tends to be all-consuming. But even though business will dominate your time and energy in the first few years of starting your business, it needs to be kept in perspective. Be clear about why your business exists and how it serves the overall purpose of your life.

Please use the following questions to reflect on the purpose of your life. What are your dreams for your life? What is important to you (your values)? What brings you fulfillment? What is the Lord putting on your heart to do with your life? Why are you here? If you had to write down the purpose of your life, what would it be? What are the top three things you want to accomplish before you die? Ask God to guide you as you reflect and write. Also, get input from your parents and church leaders who know you well.

Now that you've spent some initial time pondering this, come back to it every few months to see it with fresh eyes, tweaking it as you get to know yourself better and as God brings new experiences your way that shape you.

Ask yourself (*Adapt* business to your life plan):

How might business fit in with my life purpose and goals?

_____

_____

Is the timing right?

_____

_____

Why do I want to start a business?

_____

_____

Is the reason strong enough to sustain me through the inevitable hardships I'll face? Pray about whether God is truly calling me into business.

_____

_____

Meditate on these scriptures (*Adapt* business to your life plan):

Secondary things find their purpose in relation to primary things. Matthew 6:33 (NIV): *"But seek first his kingdom and his righteousness, and all these things will be given to you as well."*

Lesson 1G: *Make* time work for you

Follow expert advice (*Make* time work for you):

Business will demand most of your time in the beginning years so count the cost and decide what you're willing to give up. Learn to manage your time more effectively.

With only 24 hours in each day, time is scarce and valuable. The Apostle Paul exhorts us to "make the most of every opportunity" (Ephesians 5:16). If you aren't proactive in how you use your time, the overwhelming demands of starting a business will stress you to your limits. If you add business to your life, you'll need to subtract something – or likely several somethings! Try not to subtract too much sleep as you need it to stay mentally and physically sharp – which you'll definitely need. Same with exercising, eating healthy foods, investing in family and friends, and practicing a weekly

Sabbath to be renewed and to express your dependence on God. So, what will you give up? You'll need to learn to say "no" and "not now" to both time wasters and otherwise good opportunities. "Good is the enemy of great." (Collins, 2011, p.1)

The key to choosing what to do with your time is discerning the difference between what is urgent and what is important. Urgent matters may or may not be important. Some interruptions, calls, emails, and emergencies are important to others, but do they fit into what God has called you to do – the purposes of your life and business? The answer is sometimes "yes" and is an opportunity to "deny yourself" to serve others and fulfill your obligations to your family. Other times, you must risk the displeasure of others so you can stay focused on what is most important. At work, this should be defined by the top goals that help advance the vision and mission of your business. Often these big goals are longer term, so they seem less urgent today. But if you don't take small steps toward them on a regular basis, you may never reach them. "How do you eat an elephant?" "One bite at a time!"

Another piece of wisdom for managing time is to block of several hours of uninterrupted time for important things. I'm doing this right now. I'm on a weeklong trip to start writing this book. Finishing other things before I left home and being unplugged from daily tasks and interruptions is allowing me to think and write these very words. This is important because of how God wired our brains. We cannot truly multi-task and studies show it takes a lot of mental time and energy to keep transitioning back and forth between different tasks. Our brains do our best work when we're able to focus on only one thing. (Medina, 2014, p.115) So, decide in advance which big goals and tasks you should schedule into your week, then fit the lesser important things in around them. "The key is not to prioritize what's on your schedule, but to schedule your priorities" (Covey, 1989, p. 161). Like money, time will slip away if you don't tell it where to go. So, use a schedule for your time like you use a budget for your money.

 Ask yourself (*Make* time work for you):

What will I sacrifice to make time to build a business?

_____

_____

What are the chronic time-wasters (neither productive nor restorative) that I can cut out of my life?

_____

_____

What are some urgent demands on my time that are not truly important?

_____

_____

How can I carve out large chunks of uninterrupted time in my week to do important things to build my business?

_____

_____

Meditate on these scriptures (*Make time work for you*):

Time is a precious gift to steward. Ephesians 5:15-16 (NIV): *"Be very careful, then, how you live—not as unwise but as wise, making the most of every opportunity, because the days are evil."*

The brevity of life reveals the value of time. Psalm 90:12 (NIV): *"Teach us to number our days, that we may gain a heart of wisdom."*

 Observe teens who follow advice:

Once Alejandro and Maria ordered their food and settled into their seats, Alejandro earnestly prayed. He thanked God for their meal and asked for guidance on the next steps. Maria pulled out her phone to take notes. "Alright Alejandro, let's think this through. Why would God call us to start our own tortilleria? I want to write down all the pros and cons before we get started."

Alejandro started talking quickly:

"First, you love to cook. Flavors, spices, textures — your grandmother taught you all the secrets. Since you were a little girl, you've worked hard at home and school. Everyone is always asking you if they can come over for dinner. You're the best cook I know!

"Second, I love to get a deal. I will get us the best prices on ingredients, on the equipment, on the rent. At school, all of the lessons on money have been my favorites. And my uncle has taught me how to talk to people. He's always smiling, asking for a better price, getting the store to throw in something else for free. I can do what he does!

"Third, we are hard workers. We don't need to waste time on soccer, TV, or our cellphones. We want a better life. And if we do this right, we can help others out. We can hire Mario and many others. People at our church need good jobs!"

Maria paused to think. Then she said, "But we are so young! How will we protect ourselves from the gangs? What if no one wants to buy our tortillas? We have to think about the challenges too!"

Alejandro gave Maria one of his famous smiles. "You heard the sermon at church, right? The pastor said we have to be strong and take courage, just like Joshua. You look out for the problems; I will look for the solutions. We'll be a team. I know we can do this together!"

 Avoid **these top five mistakes:**

1. Not intentionally growing in both character and skills.
2. Learning to make a product but not grow a business.
3. Underestimating how demanding business will be on your time and energy.
4. Thinking that business is about greed and less honorable than professions that seem more spiritual.
5. Not writing down your life purpose and goals.

Form these top five habits:

1. Try different types of work to see what engages your talents and blesses others.
2. Build trusting, long-term relationships in every part of your life.
3. Take lots of small risks knowing that failure doesn't diminish your identity as a child of God.
4. Do projects that take a long time (months or years) to complete.
5. Read and write every day.

 Follow this real-life Honduran example:

Fausto Varela is the best example we know of in any country of someone who follows this module's advice to be a lifelong learner. As a thin man with an eager demeanor and slightly wild curls in his hair, he even looks hungry for knowledge! He certainly devours books on personal growth and business quicker than anyone else we know. He puts what he learns into practice and amazing results follow. Here is his story in his own words (with editing by Carol McGehe). Please listen for echoes of the expert advice from this module, especially "grow in character" and "develop your business skills."

Fausto with his family

Fausto Varela: *"I recall having business ideas from the age of 9-years-old. When I visited my grandmother one summer and saw her mango tree, I said to myself, 'If only I could take all these mangos back home, slice them, and add salt and spices, I could make a lot of money selling them at school.' So I did. It went so well that the school authorities shut down my business because I was in competition with the school's cafeteria! So I had a lot of extra spiced mango to eat myself. All my wild business ideas often got me into trouble, especially with my teachers. Only when I met my wife Jackie did I find someone who would listen to my ideas, without laughing or rolling her eyes, and dream big dreams with me.*

Since Jackie and I are both musicians, my next attempt at becoming an entrepreneur was to create a business with Jackie that would help young musicians here in Honduras perform in concerts. I was hoping a business would help get me out of the debt that was worrying me. Even though being a student was my only "job", I had borrowed money to go to a music festival, without realizing that when I got back, I wouldn't have a job to help pay back the loan. I had no idea how to manage money.

One day soon after the concert, I noticed a book on personal finances and business that I had given to my dad as a gift. Since he had never read it, I snatched it up. While waiting for a bus, I read five entire chapters and found exactly the information I needed! I was hungry for knowledge. I finally got out of debt with small business ideas and playing gigs and small concerts here and there.

With the help of my father-in-law who encouraged us to trust God to guide our business decisions, we began to obey Proverbs 3:5 which says to 'Trust in the Lord with all your heart and lean not on your own understanding; in all your ways submit to Him, and He will make your paths straight.' Becoming mature entrepreneurs and creating wealth has been a constant learning process as we walk with God and let His influence sink into our hearts and minds.

We started our business on February 15 2010, under the name "Soli Deo Gloria School of Music" (which, in Latin, means "to God alone, the Glory"). We started with about seven students in a very small area inside the church we attend. We kept learning and we grew to 12, and then 20 students. After making some changes in our systems and hiring additional teachers, we grew to 27 students.

At this point in our growth, I heard Evan Keller (director of Creating Jobs Inc and lead author of this book) *speak at a seminar which led to us becoming part of the mentoring program Creating Jobs Inc does in partnership with our church Iglesia Cristiana Vida Abundante. We participated in our first mentoring session with Evan Keller and Larry McGehe in February 2013. That year, because of the mentoring program, we doubled the number of students from what was then 44, to 88!*

In order to grow our business, we have we had to learn about a lot of topics that have nothing to do with music, such as human relations, public relations, finance, marketing, sales, accounting, legal procedures, production, leadership, emotional intelligence, and even how to look good on camera! Truthfully, the list never ends. God has been faithful, and we are really enjoying this continuous learning process. (My high school teachers would be shocked to hear me say that!)

After hearing another wise businessman, Jim Rohn, say: 'Income seldom exceeds personal development,' (https://youtu.be/jnBdNkkceZw) we knew we needed to be proactive and develop a plan for our personal improvement. In our efforts to become successful entrepreneurs, we've had to continually learn more and more. Interestingly, the more we study, the more we realize how much we don't know! We continue to meet with my father-in-law, but we have also sought out other mentors who can help in specific areas. We attend seminars, read like crazy, and listen to valuable recordings on personal development.

Today, as I tell you this story, our school currently serves more than 120 students and keeps growing as we keep learning. Soli Deo Gloria!"

You can see how Fausto and Jackie perfectly live out this module's advice to diligently grow both their character and their business skills. Even their superb musical talents show that they're committed to developing what God has given them. Their identity in Christ gives them confidence to make bold strides in business. They understand the biblical purpose of business to meet the needs of the world, including the beautiful music they help their students to make!

Do with your group:

Split into groups of 3-4 with half of the groups allowed to use paper and pencil while the other groups cannot. Each group must perform this task: Add up the total number of edges on a: square, cube, triangle, and three-sided pyramid. Record the time it takes for each group to complete the task. Did the groups with paper and pencil work faster and why? How does writing things down help our brains work better?

Teacher's guide: The numerical answer is: 4+12+3+6=25. Drawing helps us visualize, and writing numbers and words allows our brains to switch focus from short-term memory to reasoning. When thoughts are written down, we can better tie them together, improve the wording, and further develop and explain ideas. When we make a habit of writing, just picking up a pen or keyboard can trigger the brain that it's time to get creative!

 Apply this module with:

PRAYER – Ask God for a deeper revelation of who I am as an object of God's immeasurable love. Ask God to show me more of the talents he's given me. Ask God to change my character to better reflect Jesus. Ask God whose character I should seek to emulate. Ask God to show me how my skills intersect the needs of his world. Ask God to show me whether He is calling me into business.

RESEARCH – Take a personality assessment such as StrengthsFinder, Meyers-Briggs, or DISC. Research needed skills and accreditations and how to get them.

CREATIVITY – Write down a risk I can take to develop my God-given talents. Begin a new habit that God could use to shape my character. Write my life purpose, and then get feedback on it.

ACTION – Buy a notebook to keep all my business notes in. Or find a quick way to access my business ideas on my electronic device. In your notebook, take time to write your reflections on the following questions suggested by Warren Buffett (the second wealthiest person in the world): Who do you want to be like? Who is repulsive to you? Write down the actions and underlying character traits you see in both. Decide which traits you want to grow into and which you want to grow out of. Andrés Panasiuk suggests that you make a list of what you have (opportunities, relationships, and talents) and ask God how he wants to use them. (Buffett, Panasiuk, 2015)

CUSTOMERS – Ask potential customers which of the above character traits are most important to them in the people they do business with.

MENTORS – Ask them to assess my character and strengths. Identify which traits in my mentors that I want to emulate and ask how they grew in those areas.

MONEY – Use a small amount of money to make someone smile this week then ponder what this taught me about money as a tool.

TIME – Choose one of this module's Top 5 Habits to start practicing. Record and time each activity I do over a 24 hour period, then write what surprised me about how I use my time and which activities were urgent and/or important. Decide what time-wasters to reduce or eliminate from my week. Try keeping a Sabbath day each week. Decide what sacrifices I would have to make if I start a business.

 ## *Practice* values of Compassion International:

Integrity – Being Christ-like in both your thoughts and actions is what having integrity is all about. With God's power, you can grow in character as this module discusses. This will make both your business and personal relationships healthier and more enjoyable.

Excellence –Working hard to develop your skills reflects God's own "very good" work. Growing the seed of talent God planted in you honors him as much as the worship you offer at church!

Stewardship – God's gift of time is a priceless treasure that is easily taken for granted. While you have the breath of life in you, remember that you are representing God. So use your time wisely to glorify him.

Dignity – Because work is a good gift from God, doing a good job gives you a sense of purpose. When you see how your work is part of loving your neighbors, it reminds you who you are – a son or daughter of a God who is love.

Evaluate the teen business:

Review your notes on this module. Now, imagine you are a professional business coach!

- What are Alejandro and Maria doing right as they prepare to start their tortilleria?
- What lessons do they need to learn?
- What advice would you give them so they get off to a good start?

Sum it up:

This module has painted the picture for you of what a mature entrepreneur is like. Ponder whether this is who you want to be. How far along are you and how will you grow further? Leading yourself well is the first step toward being someone others will want to follow.

Use your *Start*Book Plan:

Now that you've completed this module, please fill out your *Start*Book Plan on the next page. Think about what you've learned and choose the important goal for you to apply this module to your business over the next 12 months. Write down your goal, three actions to accomplish it, and dates to complete each one. Refer to your *Start*Book Plan often as a tool to grow your business.

Start**Book** Plan

1. You

Module snapshot: Learn what makes a mature entrepreneur. Assess yourself and plan to grow.

My #1 "You" goal for the next 12 months:

My top 3 action steps to accomplish this goal:

1.

Today's date: _____ Target completion date: _____ Actual completion date: _____

2.

Today's date: _____ Target completion date: _____ Actual completion date: _____

3.

Today's date: _____ Target completion date: _____ Actual completion date: _____

2. Solution

Module snapshot: Create a unique solution to a real problem, letting your customers' input shape your product or service. Build your business identity around that solution and design systems to produce your product efficiently and safely.

Module 2: SOLUTION

 Consider module snapshot: Create a unique solution to a real problem, letting your customers' input shape your product or service. Build your business identity around that solution and design systems to produce your product efficiently and safely.

 Observe teens who need advice:

After talking with a mentor, Alejandro and Maria decided to ask everyone they knew what made the perfect tortilla. They wrote each response down in notepads, then met two days later to share what they had heard. The main ideas were: fresh, hot, cheap, crispy/soft, not sweet, no funky smells, a little puffy, salty.

"But Alejandro, I already know all of this!" complained Maria. "Why are we wasting our time asking people what they like? Like you said, I'm the best cook you know! What's the point? Let's just get started!"

Lesson 2A: *Choose* a problem to solve

 Follow expert advice (*Choose* a problem to solve):

Entrepreneurs are problem solvers and need-meeters. Listen for what you and others complain about. Look for "wants" as well as "needs" in your community and talk to as many people as you can about their experience with this problem. Make a list of these problems and brainstorm possible solutions with your friends, family, and mentors – writing down your best ideas (of course!). If people already pay for some type of solution to your chosen problem, there's a better chance it's important enough to solve. Look for improvements or alternatives to those existing solutions. Study their strengths and weaknesses.

Choose one of the problems you've identified that (1) bother enough people to build a business on, (2) you have found a great solution for, and (3) you can equip yourself to solve in the near future. Even if you've successfully identified the exact solution that hordes of people would part with their money for, there's no guarantee that you are the best person to provide it. You may or may not have the skills, tools, capital, materials or knowledge to successfully produce it. It's okay to learn as you go, but be sure you choose something you can be competitive at fairly quickly. Be ambitious and realistic *at the same time!*

Ask yourself (*Choose* a problem to solve):

What are some problems people complain about?

_____

_____

_____

What are some possible solutions?

_____

_____

_____

How are these problems currently being addressed?

_____

_____

_____

How satisfying are the current solutions?

_____

_____

_____

What problem have I found an innovative solution for?

_____

_____

_____

Do I have the skills and tools to produce it?

_____

_____

 ### *Meditate* on these scriptures (*Choose* a problem to solve):

Solving a community problem builds strong relationships with many neighbors. Mark 12:31 (NIV): *"'Love your neighbor as yourself.' There is no commandment greater than these."*

Lesson 2B: *Find* your unique value

 ### *Follow* expert advice (*Find* your unique value):

Explore whether there is any advantage you'd have in producing the needed solution, such as an inexpensive source of quality materials or tools. For Ruy Gomez Gutierrez, it's a quality product at a lower price – which is hard to pull off. He's the owner of Signia in Queretaro, Mexico. He searched long and hard until he found a local supplier of aluminum coil to produce large channel letters for his customer's signs. When he found a local source of aluminum, he was able to serve his customers a lot faster without all the cumbersome import procedures. Best yet, he reduced his material cost by 85%! He was able to lower his prices and become the leading supplier of this type of signage in his region, while still increasing his profit margin substantially. He was able to support his local economy and reduce wasteful transportation costs.

Ruy in center, with Creating Jobs Inc mentors Manny De La Vega to his right and Evan Keller to his left

Maybe your advantage is that your location is close to your customers. Maybe a friend or family member is offering you a rent-free location for a period of time. Maybe you have superior skills, better processes, a secret recipe, more professional communication, or more attentive customer service.

Ask yourself (*Find* your unique value):

What advantages do I have over my competitors?

_____

_____

How can I put those to work to build my business and please my customers?

_____

_____

 ### *Meditate* on these scriptures (*Find* your unique value):

It is deeply fulfilling to do what you're best at to serve others. 1 Peter 4:10 (NIV): *"Each of you should use whatever gift you have received to serve others, as faithful stewards of God's grace in its various forms."*

A faithful steward puts God's talents to work to create more value. Matthew 25:20-21 (NIV): *"The man who had received five bags of gold brought the other five. 'Master,' he said, 'you entrusted me with five bags of gold. See, I have gained five more.'*

"His master replied, 'Well done, good and faithful servant! You have been faithful with a few things; I will put you in charge of many things. Come and share your master's happiness!'"

Lesson 2C: *Research* whether customers would pay for your chosen solution

 Follow expert advice (*Research* whether customers would pay for your chosen solution):

Before you spend much time and money developing your product, ask hundreds of people which possible solutions they'd prefer and how much they'd be willing to pay for them. It's not good enough that they like your ideas; they must be willing to purchase them at a price you're able to profitably offer instead of what is currently available. 42% of new businesses fail because there is not enough demand for the solutions they offer. According to *Fortune Magazine*, this is the *biggest* reason new businesses fail! (Griffith, 2016)

How are you any different?

Ask yourself (*Research* whether customers would pay for your chosen solution):

Which solution do people really want – my proposal or one that's already available?

_____

_____

Do enough people *really* want what I offer?

_____

_____

If they like my idea, how much are they willing to pay for it?

_____

_____

Can I produce it for 20-50% less than that?

_____

_____

Why would they buy from me?

_____

_____

How many potential customers have said they would buy from me at a profitable price?

_____

_____

Meditate on these scriptures (*Research* whether customers would pay for your chosen solution):

It is human nature to overestimate the value of your own ideas and work. Romans 12:3 (NIV): *"For by the grace given me I say to every one of you: Do not think of yourself more highly than you ought, but rather think of yourself with sober judgment, in accordance with the faith God has distributed to each of you."*

Lesson 2D: *Design* your solution with your customers' input

Follow expert advice (*Design* your solution with your customers' input):

Think and work night and day to make your product amazing. But don't keep it all secret until you think it's perfect, since what you like isn't always what your customers like. To stay in touch with what is important to them, show it to several of them and get their feedback every time you make an improvement or have a new idea. This way your customers have a part in designing products they will buy. Who doesn't want something made with them in mind? That's why we asked Honduran teenagers for feedback on this book before creating the final version. "Then after your customers actually purchase and use your product, their feedback will be even more helpful to you" (Lee Murray).

If you're a guy, get a girl's perspective and vice versa. Together, we reflect the image of God who told us to create and rule together, so it makes perfect sense that we would design better products and services as a team. We intentionally did this when building our team of authors to write this book for you.

 Ask yourself (*Design* your solution with your customers' input):

Who are 10 people who may be interested in my product or service?

_____

_____

Would they be willing to give me feedback as I design it?

_____

_____

Which members of the opposite sex could give me input on blind spots in my product design?

_____

_____

 Meditate on these scriptures (*Design your solution with your customers' input*):

Inviting much feedback from actual users is the best way to assess your products. Proverbs 15:22 (NIV): *"Plans fail for lack of counsel, but with many advisers they succeed.*

"

Lesson 2E: *Produce* your solution efficiently

Follow export advice (*Produce* your solution efficiently):

Constantly work to provide your product or service with less waste of time and materials. Wasteful production is a quick way to go out of business, since neither you nor your customer wants to pay for waste: you'll make no money with a low price and you'll lose customers with too high of a price. A good business creates value – doing a lot with a little. This is a faint but true reflection of your Creator who alone can create out of absolutely nothing. You combine things He's created with your ideas and effort (which are also gifts from Him) to make something new. What a privilege! If you can find ways to do more with less, you'll make more money and you can offer a competitive price to your customers. Everyone's happy! That's how business should be – every transaction is good for both parties.

Ask yourself (*Produce* your solution efficiently):

What types of waste are raising the cost of making my product?

_____

_____

How can I reduce this waste?

_____

_____

Am I able to make my product efficiently enough to sell at the same cost as my competitors' products?

_____

_____

Or are my solutions so superior that customers are willing to pay more for them?

_____

_____

What are the key ingredients that create value for my customers?

_____

_____

 Meditate on these scriptures (*Produce* your solution efficiently):

Working smarter brings more for your effort. Ecclesiastes 10:10 (ESV): *"If the iron is blunt, and one does not sharpen the edge, he must use more strength, but wisdom helps one to succeed."*

Lesson 2F: *Improve* by using systems

 Follow expert advice (*Improve* by using systems):

As you find efficient ways to produce your products and services, write down the steps in the order they happen so that you and your employees can do it with excellence every time. Written systems help your employees do things your way, so train them and get their feedback to update your systems at least twice a year. Good systems can also make your workplace more orderly and safe. If your employees use your systems to produce your products, customers will appreciate receiving predictable products. When they know your products will be high quality every time, it builds trust in you and keeps them coming back. Systems for producing your solution may include: recipes, assembly instructions, safety procedures, supply purchasing schedule, production schedule, quality control process, and shipping steps.

Ask yourself (*Improve* by using systems):

What are the best steps to create my product?

_____

_____

What systems will boost order, efficiency, and safety?

_____

_____

How will I communicate and train my employees to use my production system?

_____

_____

How often will I update my production system with feedback from my employees?

_____

_____

Do my customers experience consistent level of quality?

_____

_____

 Meditate on these scriptures (*Improve* by using systems):

God wants all things done in order. 1 Corinthians 14:33 (NIV): *"For God is not a God of disorder but of peace—as in all the congregations of the Lord's people."*

Lesson 2G: *Create* your business identity to share your solution:

 Follow expert advice (*Create* your business identity to share your solution):

Now that you know what your customers want, choose a business name, tagline, and logo that clearly communicate the solution you've created for them. With a quick glance at your logo, people should be able to tell what you can do to help them. Make it about *them*, not you. So, name your business after your solution, not yourself! Choose a tagline that isn't a silly rhyme; people want to do business with professionals not clowns. Make it short and let it express the unique value you provide. Make your logo readable at small sizes and at fast speeds. Keep the graphics simple and able to powerfully communicate in a single glance. Your logo can't explain everything about your business – it only gives a good first taste. "Entrepreneurs try to say too much with their logos and end up saying nothing because they fail to capture and keep attention." (Keller, 2015, p.73) "If you say three things, you don't say anything." (Heath & Heath, 2008, p.33)

 ### *Ask* yourself (*Create* your business identity to share your solution):

What business name would best communicate my solution, be one to three words long, and be surprising?

_____

_____

What tagline would capture the flavor of my solution in a single, non-silly phrase?

_____

_____

What logo font and graphics would give the best snapshot of my business?

Meditate on these scriptures (*Create your business identity to share your solution*):

Addressing customer needs in your branding puts them first. Philippians 2:3-4 (NIV): "*Do nothing out of selfish ambition or vain conceit. Rather, in humility value others above yourselves, not looking to your own interests but each of you to the interests of the others.*"

Observe teens who follow advice:

"Ok, Maria, you have a point." said Alejandro. "You know how to make the best tortillas! So let's ask our friends some better questions. To get the answers we really need to succeed."

Maria was discouraged from wasting two days asking people how to cook tortillas — something she already knew how to do! "I don't know. Like what?" she said.

Alejandro thought for a minute. "Why don't we ask our friends *when* they buy tortillas and *why* they buy tortillas?" Maria said, "But I think it is just a meal. You get it for breakfast, or lunch, or dinner, or late at night. So what? How will that help?"

They both sat in silence, trying to figure out how to do something better than the thousands of other tortillerias in their city. It seemed like all the good ideas were already taken.

Finally Maria said, "Ok, Alejandro, I have an idea. Let's ask people what their *dream tortilleria* would be like. The Best Ever. Their Favorite. I don't want to make hundreds of the same cheap, boring tortillas, starting before the sun comes up, until my back gives out. I want to do something new and amazing."

"That's it!" Alejandro exclaimed. "If we find out what people wish they could get at a tortilleria, but can't, then we can be the only ones in town! Everyone will be talking about our new ideas and flavors. We'll be a hit! Let's try it."

 Avoid these top five mistakes:

1. Assuming that everyone will want your product or service enough to pay for it.
2. Believing your product is superior to most others with very little evidence to prove it.
3. Choosing a business name that doesn't communicate the solution you offer, including naming it after yourself.
4. Making a logo too detailed so it has low visual impact.
5. Making a tagline cute instead of professional.

Form these top five habits:

1. Rather than trying to perfect a product in secret, get feedback from customers throughout the design process.
2. Continually improve your products.
3. Break your processes into steps and write them down.
4. Improve your processes four times a year.
5. Regularly look for waste to eliminate.

 Follow this real-life Honduran example:

Even though he is quite friendly, Saul Contreras will look you steadily in the eye as if he can see into your soul! He is dedicated to his wife and two young sons, his church and its business ministry that he leads. Saul is also quite serious about constantly analyzing and improving his business. He applied that determination to find a real need and design a great solution that people were willing to pay for. Here's his story in his own words as told to Odile Perez.

Saul with his wife

Saul Contreras: *"The idea for my company arose when I saw a need that was not being met. At that time I frequently visited a small plumbing company owned by ex-father-in-law and I realized that many of his customers were calling to request cleaning and treatment service for their drinking water storage tanks. However, his company did not have the capacity to solve this problem.*

To further explore this problem, I began to do market research and found that there was only one company that offered these services and that most of the demand came from the upper middle class. To have a total clarity of the need, with my ex-father-in-law's permission, I contacted hundreds of his clients to define their needs. Based on their answers, I designed a solution that offered a professional and trustworthy service. In 2001, I started a business called Ser Móvil to provide cleaning services, pest control and wastewater treatment.

From the beginning, I was determined to bring unique value to my customers. In order to set ourselves apart in the market, we use modern equipment, biodegradable detergents and products that are environmentally safe. By offering high quality products and having uniformed and professional employees, we have differentiated ourselves from other companies and thus, created our niche. To keep our competitive advantage, we constantly improve our systems and survey our customers to ensure customer satisfaction. This has allowed us to continue grow not only in Tegucigalpa but also in other cities, acquire a new and bigger location, buy new work vehicles and employ more staff.

As I grew in my relationship to God, I realized that he cares about how we care for the Earth he's entrusted to us. By providing environmentally safe products that won't harm my customers, God is pleased and I am a faithful stewards of his. To make it clearer to clients who we are and what we offer, we changed our business name in 2017 from Ser Móvil to Eco-Solutions. Our focus is to continue to identify environmental needs and offer solutions that keep our customers coming back to us."

Instead of starting with a hobby he enjoyed, Saul first looked for what other people wanted that wasn't currently available. That's the sign of a true entrepreneur. He sought out customer feedback to both design and improve his services. Saul found out what people couldn't find from his competitors to create his company's unique value. Notice that Saul is so focused on meeting customer needs that even his business name includes the word "solutions" as well as the type of solutions ("eco") that his customers want!

Do with your group:

After learning from the area's best shoemaker, Lily Flores is starting a business to make shoes for the residents of Flor del Campo. It is a lower income neighborhood, which wants shoes in the latest style at affordable prices. The neighborhood is built on a steep hillside above a winding river and a long bridge. What is a good name and tagline for her business? List the group's top three ideas for each, then vote on which is the best. How well does your chosen name and tagline follow the expert advice section entitled: "Create your business identity to share your solution" (lesson 2G)?

Teacher's guide: Please familiarize yourself with the expert advice section mentioned above which emphasizes choosing a business name that is more about the customer than about the entrepreneur. It advises choosing a tagline that shares one's unique value in a professional way.

 Apply this module with:

PRAYER – Ask God to show me which problems he wants me to solve and seek his creativity in doing so.

RESEARCH – Learn about problems people have.

CREATIVITY – Write down three problems that interest me and five potential solutions for each. Write a step-by-step system to produce my product. Write five business names, five taglines, and five logo concepts.

ACTION – Get together with friends interested in business to brainstorm possible solutions.

CUSTOMERS – Ask lots of potential customers if they like my solution and how much they would pay for it. Get input from them on product design.

MENTORS – Ask for their honest opinion about how many people will want my solution enough to pay good money for it.

MONEY – Write down every purchase I make this week, what problem each solves, and how that solution is better than other available options.

TIME – Block out a chunk of time to think about and write down possible solutions. Block out time to ask customers for feedback on possible solutions.

 ### *Practice* values of Compassion International:

Integrity – When you live out your tagline every day, you are who you say you are. This helps customers trust you.

Excellence – Using systems helps you make your products at the same level of quality every time. Both of these habits help you to keep improving day by day, which is another faint reflection of God's perfection.

Stewardship – Since God's creation is good, you shouldn't waste it.

You honor God when you combine the skills, time, and tools he's given you to create a useful solution. You're imitating God by bringing things he's created to their full potential.

Dignity – When you respect the needs of your customers, you honor their God-given dignity. And when you offer unique value to your neighbors, you show that God has designed you as a unique person.

Evaluate the teen business:

Review your notes on this module. As a professional business coach, imagine you are sitting down to give feedback to Alejandro and Maria on their initial research efforts.

- What could Alejandro and Maria do to gain more valuable insights from their community?
- How would you encourage them?
- What questions would you ask them?
- What ideas would you recommend they consider trying?

Sum it up:

What a joy to be part of God's answer to prayers for daily bread! Through you, He provides people with products, services, and jobs that help them to thrive. Imitate your Creator by solving problems and creating something new that is beautiful and useful.

Use your *Start*Book Plan:

Now that you've completed this module, please fill out your *Start*Book Plan on the next page. Think about what you've learned and choose the most important goal for you to apply this module to your business over the next 12 months. Write down your goal, three actions to accomplish it, and dates to complete each one. Refer to your *Start*Book Plan often as a tool to grow your business.

*Start*Book Plan

2. Solution

Module snapshot: Create a unique solution to a real problem, letting your customers' input shape your product or service. Build your business identity around that solution and design systems to produce your product efficiently and safely.

My #1 "Solution" goal for the next 12 months:

My top 3 action steps to accomplish this goal:

1.

Today's date: _____ Target completion date: _____ Actual completion date: _____

2.

Today's date: _____ Target completion date: _____ Actual completion date: _____

3.

Today's date: _____ Target completion date: _____ Actual completion date: _____

3. People

Module snapshot: Appreciate and learn from these groups of people who are vital to your success. Build trusting win-win relationships with them.

Module 3: PEOPLE

 Consider module snapshot: Appreciate and learn from these groups of people who are vital to your success. Build trusting win-win relationships with them.

 Observe teens who need advice:

It didn't take much for Alejandro to lose his temper. As he talked with Maria, he got up from his seat and started to furiously pace around the room. "I can't believe it! We came up with this great idea to create the dream tortilleria, we went around asking everyone about it, but before we've even opened for business, someone stole our ideas! Now the tortilleria across from our school has 'The Dream' tortilla for sale."

Maria was quiet. She was upset too, but didn't see the point of yelling about it. "Alejandro, it *is* really bad. Maybe we need another great idea. I don't know what to do, but shouting at the walls won't fix our problem."

Alejandro took a deep breath. "Maria, okay, okay, okay. Let's pray. And then let's figure out what to do."

Lesson 3A: *Treat* people according to their God-given dignity

 Follow expert advice (*Treat* people according to their God-given dignity):

Since God created people in his own image, they matter to God above all else. Since God defines our reality, we too must highly value people and treat them in ways that honor their God-given dignity. Care for *them* rather than just what you can gain *from* them. Respect their time, family responsibilities, and their work – even if they have a low-skilled role. Be fair in your financial relations with them. Since how you handle money reveals your heart, steer your heart by being generous. Remember that Jesus summed up God's entire law in the command to love God and love your neighbor (Mark 12:31). He also taught and demonstrated that a primary way to love God is *by* loving our neighbor.

 Ask yourself (*Treat* people according to their God-given dignity):

How do I see people differently than God does?

_____

_____

Who do I treat more like a machine than a person?

_____

_____

Who will I ask to forgive me?

_____

_____

How can I better show love to others with my time, money, and words?

_____

_____

 Meditate on these scriptures (_Treat_ people according to their God-given dignity):

Putting yourself in others' shoes leads to win-win relationships. Matthew 7:12(NIV): _"So in everything, do to others what you would have them do to you, for this sums up the Law and the Prophets."_

Christ's high standard for relationship applies to your business. Mark 12:31 (NIV): _"'Love your neighbor as yourself.' There is no commandment greater than these."_

The cross increases the dignity of all you encounter. 2 Corinthians 5:14 (NIV): *"For Christ's love compels us, because we are convinced that one died for all, and therefore all died."*

Knowing God will motivate you to be fair with your employees and advocate for the vulnerable. Jeremiah 22:13-16 (NIV): *"Woe to him who builds his palace by unrighteousness, his upper rooms by injustice, making his own people work for nothing, not paying them for their labor. He says, 'I will build myself a great palace with spacious upper rooms.' So he makes large windows in it, panels it with cedar and decorates it in red. Does it make you a king to have more and more cedar? Did not your father have food and drink? He did what was right and just, so all went well with him. He defended the cause of the poor and needy, and so all went well. Is that not what it means to know me?" declares the LORD."*

Lesson 3B: *Find* the best suppliers

Follow expert advice (*Find* the best suppliers):

If you bake bread, you'll need to buy flour and yeast. Before you buy from someone, ask other buyers about their experience with this person then interview the person yourself. Start with a small order to see if they are trustworthy, while also doing what you say you'll do. As you earn their trust, you prove that you are a low-risk customer. Because of this, they may extend better terms (credit, speed, and price) to you. Always have two different suppliers for each type of material you buy. Make the best one your primary supplier, and buy less from your secondary supplier. This keeps them honest and allows them to compete for your business. If your primary supplier of yeast is late on his deliveries or raises his prices too much without good cause, make your other supplier the primary one.

 Ask yourself (*Find* the best suppliers):

What will I need to buy in order to create my products and get them to my customers?

_____

_____

Who will I buy these supplies from?

_____

_____

Are they honest, fair, reliable, and easy to reach?

_____

_____

Do they sell quality products?

_____

_____

How will I choose a primary supplier between two people who supply the same materials?

_____

_____

What actions of mine will earn their trust?

_____

_____

When I gain it, will I ask for credit, a better price, or a quicker delivery?

_____

_____

 Meditate on these scriptures (*Find* the best suppliers):

Find more than one good supplier in case one goes bad. Ecclesiastes 11:1-2 (NIV): *"Ship your grain across the sea after many days you may receive a return. Invest in seven ventures, yes, in eight; you do not know what disaster may come upon the land."*

Lesson 3C: *Respect* and learn from your competitors:

Follow Expert Advice (*Respect* and learn from your competitors):

Find out who is the best in your industry and learn from them. Sometimes you'll observe them from afar, but in some cases you'll be able to build a friendly relationship with them. You may want to emulate their best ideas, but if you copy too much you'll lose what makes you unique!

Commit to never bad-mouth them to your customers; instead focus on how you "stand out" and let them judge others for themselves. Customers will respect you for biting your tongue and you may need a favor from a competitor some day!

It is common for business people to complain about too many competitors, but there are reasons to be thankful for them: They show you that there is a big need for the solution you offer – that's very good news! Also, they keep you "on your toes," striving for excellence to earn customers' business. If you provide top products and earn a reputation for being trustworthy, your business will grow regardless of competition.

When competitors (or customers or suppliers) mistreat you, it is an opportunity to demonstrate your faith in Jesus who tells us to love our enemies and do good to those who mistreat us (Matthew 5:44).

 Ask yourself (*Respect* and learn from your competitors):

Who are my top competitors?

_____

_____

What are their strengths and weaknesses?

_____

_____

How can I exceed what others offer?

_____

_____

What thinking and speaking about them do I need to adjust?

_____

_____

Can I honestly thank God for my competitors and wish them well?

_____

_____

What good can I do to a competitor who has harmed me?

_____

_____

 Meditate on these scriptures (*Respect and learn from your competitors*):

Even if they do you wrong, seek a positive relationship with competitors. Romans 12:17-19 (NIV): *"Do not repay anyone evil for evil. Be careful to do what is right in the eyes of everyone. If it is possible, as far as it depends on you, live at peace with everyone. Do not take revenge, my dear friends, but leave room for God's wrath, for it is written: "It is mine to avenge; I will repay," says the Lord."*

Evildoers have no lasting power over you. Proverbs 24:19-20 (NIV): *"Do not fret because of evildoers or be envious of the wicked, for the evildoer has no future hope, and the lamp of the wicked will be snuffed out."*

Lesson 3D: *Find* supporting peers

 Follow expert advice (*Find* supporting peers):

Build relationships with several other entrepreneurs who can offer each other mutual support and connections. Especially look for people in similar, but not exact industries. These people may be in your Compassion International center or in a networking group. Suppliers can be good peers to give and receive help. Building a business is a difficult venture that most people who work a regular job don't understand, so finding others who share your joys and challenges will be a Godsend.

 Ask yourself (*Find* supporting peers):

Who is at a similar stage in business as me?

_____

_____

Do I trust them and feel a personal connection with them?

_____

_____

How can I be intentional in building a supporting relationship with these peers?

_____

_____

 Meditate on these scriptures (*Find* supporting peers):

Mutual support is one way God shows his love to you and through you. Romans 12:15 (NIV): *"Rejoice with those who rejoice and weep with those who weep."*

The many burdens of business are lighter when shared. Galatians 6:2 (ESV): *"Bear one another's burdens, and so fulfill the law of Christ."*

Your gifts are meant to serve others. Romans 12:3-8 (NIV): *"For by the grace given me I say to every one of you: Do not think of yourself more highly than you ought, but rather think of yourself with sober judgment, in accordance with the faith God has distributed to each of you. For just as each of us has one body with many members, and these members do not all have the same function, so in Christ we, though many, form one body, and each member belongs to all the others. We have different gifts, according to the grace given to each of us. If your gift is prophesying, then prophesy in accordance with your faith; if it is serving, then serve; if it is teaching, then teach; 8 if it is to encourage, then give encouragement; if it is giving, then give generously; if it is to lead, do it diligently; if it is to show mercy, do it cheerfully."*

Males and females need each other. Genesis 2:18 (NIV): *"The Lord God said, 'It is not good for the man to be alone. I will make a helper suitable for him.'*

Lesson 3E: *Seek* out wise and experienced mentors

 Follow expert advice (*Seek* out wise and experienced mentors):

Find advice and encouragement from your parents, pastors, Compassion leaders, and successful entrepreneurs who run their businesses with integrity. When you ask for advice, notice whether they give you time and take an interest in you. In the initial meeting, be specific in what you ask of them, such as an hour face-to-face every three months plus an occasional short phone call as needed. Don't expect too much of their time, but if they have none for you, seek out someone else who is more available. Watch them and emulate them. Ask them how they responded when facing similar challenges and opportunities that you now face. Be grateful and seek to help them however you can. Then pass it on by sharing what you're learning with people you are a step or two ahead of in business.

Ask yourself (*Seek* out wise and experienced mentors):

Which successful entrepreneurs do I know and respect?

_____

_____

Do they show an interest in me and my business?

_____

_____

When and what should I ask from them?

_____

_____

How can I say thanks? Who can I begin to mentor?

_____

_____

Meditate on these scriptures (*Seek out wise and experienced mentors*):

Wisdom of more experienced people is essential. Proverbs 15:22 (NIV): *"Plans fail for lack of counsel, but with many advisers they succeed."*

Lesson 3F: *Be* slow to take on partners

 Follow expert advice (*Be* slow to take on partners):

Only take on partners who have equal passion for the business and are trustworthy and contribute something you cannot provide yourself. If not, you'll dilute your profits and slow down or cripple your decision-making. Only take on a partner if you're confident they will greatly accelerate the growth of your business. Before making a full commitment, do a couple of small projects together to see if they pull their weight and whether you enjoy working with them. Remember, you may see them even more than a husband or wife! You wouldn't hastily choose a spouse without first dating him/her! Learn about the differences between a working partner and an investor. If you do take on a partner or investor, make roles and financial arrangements very clear and sign a partnership agreement with the help of an attorney. Consider the advantages of growing slower through self-funding rather than taking on an investor.

 Ask yourself (*Be* slow to take on partners):

Why do I want a partner?

_____

_____

What talents should my partner have to make up for my weaknesses?

_____

_____

What candidates are available?

_____

_____

How well do I know and trust them?

_____

_____

Are they equally excited about the business?

_____

_____

What will my business look like in three years with and without this partner?

_____

_____

What type of trial period would show us whether it's a good fit?

_____

_____

What roles, ownership shares, and salaries will my partner and I have?

_____

_____

 Meditate on these scriptures (*Be* slow to take on partners):

Be wary of getting involved financially with others. Proverbs 22:26 (ESV): *"Be not one of those who gives pledges, who put up security for debts."*

Lesson 3G: *Find* good employees to grow your capacity

 Follow expert advice (*Find* good employees to grow your capacity):

To mimic God's excellence, you must offer high quality products and services. This is very hard to do at the beginning unless you have years of experience in your industry. But an experienced employee can bridge that gap. Is there a retired person you know that has some of the skills you lack? Perhaps he or she would work for you part-time to help you get started.

Even if you have the skills to launch your business alone, consider whether you want to create a job for only yourself or for others as well. Learn about the laws and consider whether you can start with subcontractors. Be on the lookout for talented, hard-working people you can trust. Ask people you already trust to recommend someone they know. Look for character, job skills and people skills.

If you hire anyone, treat them as your greatest resource and help them to constantly learn, grow, and be challenged. Happy employees lead to happy customers who lead to profitable businesses.

Business people constantly complain about employees. I've had dozens of employees either steal from me, ruin my equipment, do drugs, show up late or not at all, lie, fight with each other, be careless with customers, and make all sorts of mistakes. Some of this is unavoidable, but over time you'll get better at reading people and when you have a few good people, they will attract other good people. So, hire slow and fire fast. A bad apple can ruin the whole batch. Your good employees will think: "If the boss puts up with this behavior, why should I give my best?" And they end up doing or fixing the work of the slackers. Firing is never fun, but in the long run it's even a gift to the one you terminate, showing them they're in the wrong industry or they need to mature. You will grow thick skin as you learn to cope with the stress of employee issues.

Even with all of these hassles, the growth of your business is severely limited if you have no employees to share the load. Being a solopreneur can be a good fit for some people, but for most they've just created a job for themselves plus also have the hassle of running a business. Once your business gains a reputation as a leader in your field, you will begin to attract the best people. So, employee issues become easier over time, especially if you treat them right. This includes providing clear expectations and job descriptions, making their opinions matter, helping them develop new skills, building teamwork, showing you care about them outside of work, and paying them a little above average. Learn about their families and their dreams so they know you don't see them as mere machines that produce for you. After training them and seeing good work, trust them with real responsibility. If everything depends on you, your business is a baby!

Ask yourself (*Find* good employees to grow your capacity):

Do I plan to hire employees or do everything myself?

_____

_____

Who do I know and trust and enjoy working with?

_____

_____

Who are community leaders who can refer employees to me?

_____

_____

How will I show my employees that I care?

_____

_____

How will I develop them as leaders in my business? Are my expectations of them very clear?

 Meditate on these scriptures (*Find good employees to grow your capacity*):

Delegating responsibility grows both people and organizations. 2 Timothy 2:2 (NIV): *"And the things you have heard me say in the presence of many witnesses entrust to reliable people who will also be qualified to teach others."*

You may start out alone, but to grow you'll need to develop other leaders. Exodus 18:13-26 (NIV): *"The next day Moses took his seat to serve as judge for the people, and they stood around him from morning till evening. When his father-in-law saw all that Moses was doing for the people, he said, 'What is this you are doing for the people? Why do you alone sit as judge, while all these people stand around you from morning till evening?' Moses answered him, 'Because the people come to me to seek God's will. Whenever they have a dispute, it is brought to me, and I decide between the parties and inform them of God's decrees and instructions.' Moses' father-in-law replied, 'What you are doing is not good. You and these people who come to you will only wear yourselves out. The work is too heavy for you; you cannot handle it alone. Listen now to me and I will give you some advice, and may God be with you. You must be the people's representative before God and bring their disputes to him. Teach them his decrees and instructions, and show them the way they are to live and how they are to behave. But select capable men from all the people—men who fear God, trustworthy men who hate dishonest gain—and appoint them as officials over thousands, hundreds, fifties and tens. Have them serve as judges for the people at all times, but have them bring every difficult case to you; the simple cases they can decide themselves. That will make your load lighter, because they will share it with you. If you do this and God so commands, you will be able to stand the strain, and all these people will go home satisfied.' Moses listened to his father-in-law and did everything he said. He chose capable men from all Israel and made them leaders of the people, officials over thousands, hundreds, fifties and tens. They served as judges for the people at all times. The difficult cases they brought to Moses, but the simple ones they decided themselves."*

Observe teens who follow advice:

Alejandro and Maria decided to see their mentor, Daniel. At first, they wondered if he knew how to help them! He kept asking questions and listening, but didn't give them any advice. Finally, Daniel paused to consider all that he had heard. Then he said, "Alejandro and Maria, if a tortilleria stole the idea of two teenagers who haven't even sold a single tortilla, does that indicate you have good ideas – or bad ideas – for what people want?"

Alejandro and Maria looked at the ground. The answer was as

obvious as the dirt on their shoelaces. "Ok Daniel, I get what you're saying, but what can we do? They already took our idea!" said Maria.

Daniel had one more question. "Wait: did they take your idea – or simply validate that it is a *good* idea? Coming up with 'The Dream' tortilla is one thing, but coming up with *ten* of them – and changing them out each month – is another level. I think the two of you have the drive, the work ethic, and the desire to listen to your customers to execute this idea better than anyone else in the city."

 ## *Avoid* these top five mistakes:

1. Not keeping your promises.
2. Treating employees like machines not people.
3. Trusting too quickly by taking big risks on people you don't know.
4. Committing to a partnership without a trial period.
5. Not putting agreements into a signed contract.

 ## *Form* these top five habits:

1. Give more than you receive; look for ways to be helpful even when not asked.
2. Admit your mistakes, apologize, and show positive change

as quickly as possible.

3. Pay your suppliers quicker than expected.
4. Hire slow and fire fast.
5. Help employees see their future in your business and help them develop towards it.

 Follow this real-life Honduran example:

A young lady with a broad, welcoming smile, Maria Villela loves to delight others with her amazing cheesecakes. As someone with a genuine interest in people, she really lives out the expert advice in this module. In her own words (edited by Carol McGehe), here is how Maria built a business around people.

Maria with her husband

Maria Villela: *"After failed attempts to find a job, I decided in 2015 to create my own catering business and named it Pistacchio Catering. I started experimenting by catering to people in our church, friends, and family and very soon expanded my network of clients. I learned that surrounding myself with positive people is extremely important. Positive people influence me to make better decisions in my personal and professional life.*

After analyzing the market, I had to decide who my suppliers would be. Local bakeries, nearby grocery stores, and wholesale markets proved to be the best choice. When I was choosing people who would provide my necessary supplies, I made sure I fully researched the product I would be buying to ensure that my finished products had the best ingredients. I had to be wise and get to know my suppliers well. I took an interest in them as people, not just as suppliers. Building this type of personal relationship makes a business relationship even better. (I've even gotten some perks out of it!)

A couple of months later, I invited my boyfriend Alfredo to be my business partner. His skills as an accomplished chef added capacity to my business. Now he's not only my business partner, but my husband as well! From the very beginning, we were on the same page about how to run and grow our business. We put our focus on making every customer's experience unique and personal. We always talk to our customers as if they are members of our family. Our goal is to make them feel comfortable and assure them that we are the best choice for their event. We realize that delivery of our product does not mean that our job is over. After their events, we make time to contact our customers to inquire about their experience with us and to make sure they know we are available for any future events they may be planning.

As we continued in our business, we realized we had a lot to learn, from basic accounting to growing as leaders. Because these things are often difficult to learn on your own, we joined a community of entrepreneurs at Iglesia Cristiana Vida Abundante. We have had an amazing experience. We hear stories of success and failure, both from brand new business owners and owners with 20 years of experience. We met our mentors within this group. We stand by the idea that when you have a business, you need a mentor. Mentors are people who have lived through all the good and bad experiences in their businesses, learned from them, and have become better as a result. They are willing to share all these words of wisdom with us. We are so grateful for our mentors, because we have learned, progressed, and grown – thanks to them.

When new entrepreneurs seek out wisdom from us, our advice is: "Be humble and stay humble. You might be an amazing chef, musician, engineer, or the best-of-the-best in whatever you do, but you should never stop learning. Don't be a Mr. or Ms.-Know-It-All, because you don't know everything you need to know. Surround yourself with people that will make you grow every day. Be humble enough to listen to other people's advice and experiences. You might not do everything they say, or even agree with everything, but something good will come out of listening. Also, never stop asking good questions. Learn how to trust in other people's talents and abilities.

Most importantly, we urge others to let God be the center of their business. He will be the One in control of everything. Each one of us is His gorgeous instrument being used to complete His divine purpose. God gives our lives meaning by making our talents useful to serve other people. "

Notice how Maria sincerely values other people as people, not just for what they can do for her. She surrounds herself with people of integrity and diligence who pour into each other. She reminds me of the fact that your ability to multiply the talents God has given you depends in large part on the people you associate with.

 Do with your group:

Choose six volunteers to participate in role-plays: three to be customers and three to be motorcycle repair shop owners. Pair up each customer with a different shop owner, then hand each pair one of the below questions. Re-read to the class the expert advice in Lesson 3C ("Respect and learn from your competitors"). Then have the class witness these three conversations and ask the shop owner to follow the expert advice when answering these questions from his/her customer:

a. Customer asks: "How are you better than the other motorcycle shops around here?" Shop owner answers.

b. I heard that Pedro's shop down the street charges people to fix things that aren't really broken. Do you think that's true? Shop owner answers.

c. Why is your hourly rate higher than what MotoFix charges? Shop owner answers.

After each role-play, the teacher asks the customer: "Did the shop owner's answer make you want to buy from him/her? Why or why not?" Then the teacher asks the class: "What parts of the expert advice did the shop owner follow and not follow?"

Teacher's guide: Before the expert advice is read, please hand out the questions to all the volunteers. This will give the "customers" time to practice and give the "shop owners" time to think about how they'll answer.

Apply this module with:

PRAYER – Ask God to show me a person who I need to appreciate for who they are, not just for what they do for me. Ask God how I can show love to this person with my time and my words. Seek God about which peers and mentors to ask to help me in my business and write down their names.

RESEARCH – List supplies I'll need and suppliers to provide them. Find out who are the top competitors in my industry and identify their strengths and weaknesses.

CREATIVITY – Write down the qualifications I'd like to find in my suppliers. If I'm seeking a partner, write down the character and skills I'd like he/she to have. Write expectations or job description for an employee position I want to fill.

ACTION – Go visit a top competitor to establish a cordial relationship and learn about the industry.

CUSTOMERS – Ask potential customers what they like about my competitors.

MENTORS – Request meetings with two potential mentors and see how often they'd be willing to meet.

MONEY – Learn about how to save money from my parents and online articles.

TIME – Take extra time this week to show someone I value him/her for more than just what he/she can do for me.

 ### *Practice* values of Compassion International:

Integrity – A business partner with poor character can quickly ruin your reputation, which can sink your business. Getting to know potential partners well and starting with a trial period for your partnership will reveal their integrity or lack of it.

Excellence – You reward a supplier's commitment to quality when you buy materials from their business. Using the excellent "ingredients" they provide allows you to offer the best possible solution.

Stewardship – When you ask someone to mentor you, you are

actually giving them the gift of putting their wisdom and experience to good use. At the same time, it develops your own God-given potential.

Dignity – Instead of demonizing your competitors, respecting them honors their God-given dignity. And creating jobs for your employees gives them an opportunity to use their gifts to serve others. This affirms their sense of purpose and worth.

 Evaluate the teen business:

Put yourself in Daniel's shoes. If Alejandro and Maria came to you for advice, what would you do?

- Write down the top three questions you would ask them so you could understand their situation.

- Review the advice in this chapter. Based on what you have learned, what are the top three points of advice you would give them? Write it down.

- Think about how Alejandro and Maria are *feeling*. How would you encourage them to move ahead?

Sum it up:

Relationships are difficult and rewarding. It's what life is about, because God Himself *is* a relationship! So, commit to growing in your skills with and love for people. Give at least as much to these people as you receive from them. And rely most of all on God, who knows you best, loves you most, and provides all you need by his grace.

Use your *Start*Book Plan:

Now that you've completed this module, please fill out your *Start*Book Plan on the next page. Think about what you've learned and choose the most important goal for you to apply this module to your business over the next 12 months. Write down your goal, three actions to accomplish it, and dates to complete each one. Refer to your *Start*Book Plan often as a tool to grow your business.

*Start*Book Plan

3. People

Module snapshot: Appreciate and learn from these groups of people who are vital to your success. Build trusting win-win relationships with them.

My #1 "People" goal for the next 12 months:

My top 3 action steps to accomplish this goal:

1.

Today's date: _____ Target completion date: _____ Actual completion date: _____

2.

Today's date: _____ Target completion date: _____ Actual compl ion date: _____

3.

Today's date: _____ Target completion date: _____ Actual completion date: _____

4. Money

Module snapshot: There's never enough money for everything, so you must direct it toward your priorities. Diligently follow these best practices to control your money and patiently build wealth.

Module 4: MONEY

Consider module snapshot: There's never enough money for everything, so you must direct it toward your priorities. Diligently follow these best practices to control your money and patiently build wealth.

Observe teens who need advice:

"So Alejandro, how are we going to get started? We need to rent a shop, get a sign out front, a cash register machine, buy all the supplies for making tortillas, we need a stove, a refrigerator, pans, pots..." Maria looked worried.

"Maria, I will get us a good deal on everything. Besides, once the money starts to come in from our happy customers, we'll be able to expand our store! I'm sure we can find a way; don't look so worried." said Alejandro.

"I know you are a good negotiator – the best!" replied Maria. "But still, I think we need a financial plan if we are going to open up The Dream Tortilleria. We don't even know how much it will cost to get started."

Alejandro sighed. He knew Maria was right. "Ok, ok, you have a good point. Let's sit down and make a list of everything we think we need and how much it will cost. Then I can put my negotiating skills to the test!"

Lesson 4A: *Save* a set amount each week even if it's very small

 Follow expert advice (*Save* a set amount each week even if it's very small):

Saving money is the best way to launch and grow your business because it builds discipline and forces you to be frugal, and you appreciate equipment more when you buy it with cash not loans – not to mention all the interest you won't have to pay to the bank! Both before and after you launch, save a set amount each week into a separate account. By separate, I mean separate from your personal money and separate from your business checking account. Start now even if the amount is very small, then increase as often as able. Set a goal to reach as an emergency fund (and only withdraw for a true emergency). After you reach that, set a goal to pay for a piece of equipment you need. You'll be surprised how much you can save over time and how much satisfaction it gives to know your entire income isn't spent every week.

Ask yourself (*Save* a set amount each week even if it's very small):

Without even trying to save a tiny amount each week, why am I convinced that it is impossible to save anything from my small income?

_____

_____

Is the problem the size of my income or do I have a scarcity mentality?

_____

_____

Am I at least willing to try it for three months?

_____

_____

What are my advantages of not using a loan?

_____

_____

When and where will I open my business savings account?

_____

_____

How much will I save each week to start with?

_____

_____

How much do I plan to accumulate for my emergency fund? How much will I accumulate for my equipment fund?

_____

_____

 Meditate on these scriptures (_Save_ a set amount each week even if it's very small):

Disciplined work now will reward you later. 2 Timothy 2:3-6 (NIV): _"Join with me in suffering, like a good soldier of Christ Jesus. No one serving as a soldier gets entangled in civilian affairs, but rather tries to please his commanding officer. Similarly, anyone who competes as an athlete does not receive the victor's crown except by competing according to the rules. The hardworking farmer should be the first to receive a share of the crops."_

Steady effort towards a distant reward truly works. Proverbs 13:11 (ESV): *"Wealth gained hastily will dwindle, but whoever gatherings little by little will increase it."*

Saving for future needs is so simple and obvious that God's tiny creatures practice it. Proverbs 30:25 (NIV): *"Ants are creatures of little strength, yet they store up their food in the summer."*

Lesson 4B: *Explore* loans if necessary

 Follow expert advice (*Explore* loans if necessary):

Sometimes loans are necessary, but be sure that you spend the money on things that actually increase revenue so that you are able to pay them back (including interest and fees). Even though it may seem impossible, save and plan for the day your business will be debt-free. One way to limit debt when using a loan is to save up a large down payment and make the length of the loan as short as you can afford (shorter the loan, the higher the payment – but you'll pay less total interest).

Banks are hesitant to loan to new businesses – they want to see a track record of success. To build trust, get to know the loan officer at the bank where your checking account is – and never write a bad check. If you have collateral (equipment you're buying) and trust, your bank might take a chance on you with a small loan. If you pay it on time, you'll likely qualify for a larger loan later.

Peer lending is an option. Savings circles "loan" the "pot" to a different person at the end of each cycle. And crowdfunding websites are a popular way to raise money for unique and exciting ideas, but business loans aren't always that intriguing!

Friends and family may lend you some money if you show that you've saved up a significant amount yourself and are working hard on your business. Be careful with this option as money may change the dynamic in your relationships, especially if you aren't able to pay back as quickly as promised.

 Ask yourself (_Explore_ loans if necessary):

Do I want to explore loans or stick to savings?

_____

_____

If considering a loan, how do I know that it will increase my revenue thus providing the funds to make the loan payments?

_____

_____

Which area bank has a history of lending to people in my industry?

_____

_____

How will I begin to build trust with them?

_____

_____

Is peer lending available to me and does it fit with my business?

_____

_____

Do my parents think borrowing from family or friends is a good idea? If so, who will I ask?

_____

_____

 Meditate on these scriptures (*Explore* loans if necessary):

Understand the drawbacks as well as the benefits of borrowing money. Proverbs 22:7 (NIV): *"The rich rule over the poor, and the borrower is slave to the lender."*

Lesson 4C: *Understand* cash flow

 Follow expert advice (*Understand* cash flow):

Business cash flow is similar to personal cash flow: if you work a job, you get paychecks on a certain schedule and your bills are due on certain other dates. You've got to make sure enough of your pay is available when your bills are due. So, you already manage cash flow on a personal basis. In both life and business, no matter how big the paychecks or the sales, the bills seem to always be just as big. It takes years of disciplined effort to get ahead.

 Ask yourself (*Understand* cash flow):

Does this make sense?

_____

_____

Am I saving money so that I can bail myself out of a cash flow crisis?

_____

_____

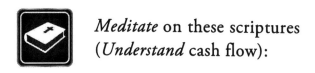

Meditate on these scriptures
(*Understand* cash flow):

No matter how many sales you make, without discipline your revenue will dwindle away. Ecclesiastes 5:11 (NIV): *"As goods increase, so do those who consume them."*

Because it ends so many businesses, the time between launch and when your business becomes self-sustaining has been nicknamed "the valley of the shadow of death." Psalm 23:4 (ESV): *"Even though I walk through the valley of the shadow of death, I will fear no evil, for you are with me."*

Lesson 4D: *Estimate* your overall business costs

Follow expert advice (*Estimate* your overall business costs):

Optimism and inexperience will likely cause you to vastly underestimate what it will cost to start and operate your business. Add up every single potential cost you can think of – then triple the total! Do this for both startup and ongoing costs, and then make a plan for how you will pay for it all until enough customers pay you. Ask one of your mentors with business experience to check your numbers and give you advice. Acquiring customers and collecting from them is much harder and slower than you can imagine, making cash flow a constant struggle for the first several years of a new business. There's a reason this period of time is called "the valley of the shadow of death!" (Psalm 23:4) Consider whether you have the frugality, creativity, and toughness to weather this ongoing source of severe stress.

 Ask yourself (*Estimate* your overall business costs):

What are all the categories of cost for the launching of my business and how much might each category cost?

_____

_____

What categories and totals of ongoing costs do you expect?

_____

_____

Which of my mentors can help me with this?

_____

_____

Do I have what it takes to handle this kind of stress?

_____

_____

Do I have the drive to pursue sales and collect the money six days a week for years?

_____

_____

 Meditate on these scriptures (*Estimate* your overall business costs):

Overestimate the cost before you begin. Luke 14:28-30 (NIV): *"Suppose one of you wants to build a tower. Won't you first sit down and estimate the cost to see if you have enough money to complete it? For if you lay the foundation and are not able to finish it, everyone who sees it will ridicule you, saying, 'This person began to build and wasn't able to finish.'"*

Lesson 4E: *Track* your top five costs every month

 Follow Expert Advice (Track your top five costs every month):

Add up all your expenses by category each month. Track your top five categories of expense each month, trying to reduce them whenever possible and find out the reasons they've gone up or down each month. After you do this for a while, you'll be able to track your spending compared to the same month (or quarter) last year and years before that. The numbers are like gauges on your car's dashboard that tell you how your business and its driver are doing. It's not good enough to just track the numbers. They do you no good unless you ask "why?" This is an important way to find and eliminate waste in your business and to see trends. Ask one of your mentors to help you read the numbers.

 Ask yourself (*Track* your top five costs every month):

How will I track all of my expenses so I can add up them up by category each month?

_____

_____

What were my top five business expenses last month?

_____

_____

How does that compare to the previous month and why?

_____

_____

If you've been tracking expenses for at least a year, how do last month's expenses compare to the same month last year?

_____

_____

Which of my mentors would have the time and expertise to help me track and interpret the numbers?

_____

_____

Meditate on these scriptures (*Track your top five costs every month*):

Don't lose touch with what is happening in your business. Proverbs 27:23 (NIV): *"Be sure you know the condition of your flocks, give careful attention to your herds."*

Lesson 4F: *Understand* fixed and variable costs

 Follow expert advice (*Understand fixed and variable costs*):

Some expenses increase when sales go up – you have to buy more flour in order to sell more bread and you use more fuel to deliver more loaves. These are called "variable costs". Other expenses are the same every month whether you sell zero or 1,000 loaves of bread – like the loan payment on your oven or rent for your building. These are called "fixed costs". If you're doing things right, your variable costs should increase slightly slower than your sales. Why? Because you may get a better price for flour when buying in larger quantities. And you should be able to map out more efficient routes, delivering more loaves per gallon of gas.

Ask yourself (*Understand* fixed and variable costs):

Do I understand the difference between fixed and variable costs?

_____

_____

If not, who can help me? Are my variable costs going up faster or slower than my sales and why?

_____

_____

 Meditate on these scriptures (*Understand* fixed and variable costs):

An increase in work brings an increase in both costs and revenue. Proverbs 14:4 (NIV): *"Where there are no oxen, the manger is empty, but from the strength of an ox come abundant harvests."*

Lesson 4G: *Keep* just enough inventory

Follow expert advice (*Keep* just enough inventory):

Keep as little in stock as possible without delaying delivery to your customers. This will keep more of your money available to pay your bills and keep you in business. Knowing what your top selling products are will help with this. Find a good way to track your inventory so you know when you're running low. If you don't, you'll disappoint customers and lose sales. Build strong relationships with suppliers so that they're willing to expedite material when you need to produce more products quickly.

Ask yourself (*Keep* just enough inventory):

What products do I sell the most and least of?

_____

_____

How many units of each do I sell each week on average?

_____

_____

Do I have too much or too little inventory?

_____

_____

How am I doing with tracking the amount I have in stock at any given moment?

_____

_____

Are my suppliers quick enough and have I given them reason to want to help me in a pinch?

_____

_____

Meditate on these scriptures (*Keep just enough inventory*):

Too much capital in inventory will cripple your business. Ecclesiastes 11:1-2 (ESV): *"Cast your bread upon the waters, for after many days you will find it again. Give portions to seven, yes to eight, for you do not know what disaster may come upon the land."*

Lesson 4H: *Get* your pricing right

 Follow expert advice (*Get* your pricing right):

Offering the lowest price is usually a horrible business strategy. There's a reason your competitors don't charge less than they do. Those who charged less than them have already gone out of business! So compete on quality, not on price. Offer a higher value (better product and service) so that you don't have to offer the lowest price, which would likely drive you out of business or keep you from offering excellence to your customers. And you must imitate the excellence of God, whose work of creation was "very good."

Set your prices above your breakeven point. Calculate it for each product you sell by using the formula below. (Lesson 4F explains fixed and variable costs). Make sure your prices are higher than your breakeven point or your business won't survive it for long.

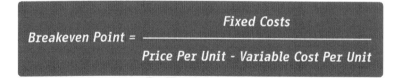

$$\text{Breakeven Point} = \frac{\text{Fixed Costs}}{\text{Price Per Unit - Variable Cost Per Unit}}$$

Too many new entrepreneurs simply copy their competitors' prices. But if you're doing things right, you're providing more value (superior product and/or customer experience), so you might need to charge more.

"Your customer, more than your competitor, needs to inform your pricing decisions." (Co.Starters). Ask your customers what they think of your pricing and do their "feet" match their words? (Sometimes they'll complain about your prices but if they still pay them, then they do see the extra value they're getting from you.)

 Ask yourself (*Get* your pricing right):

Am I competing on price or value?

_____

_____

What is my breakeven point?

_____

_____

Do my prices provide a reasonable profit margin?

_____

_____

What do my customers' words and actions say about my pricing?

_____

_____

Do I need to change any of my prices?

_____

_____

 Meditate on these scriptures (*Get* your pricing right):

Even if customers complain about your prices, their true perception shows in whether or not they still buy from you. Proverbs 20:14 (NIV): *"'It's no good, it's no good!" says the buyer-- then goes off and boasts about the purchase.'"*

Lesson 4I: *Sell* more of your more profitable products

 Follow expert advice (*Sell* more of your more profitable products):

Find out how much profit comes from each product by subtracting your breakeven point (see previous section) for a particular product from its price. Then take that number and divide it by its price. This will give you the profit margin (percentage) for that product. Do the same for each product you sell, then compare them to each other. The product with the bigger number is making you more money. Try to sell more of those and less of the others.

Price - Breakeven Point = Profit	Profit / Price = Profit Margin

 Ask yourself (*Sell* more of your more profitable products):

What is my breakeven point for each of my products?

_____

_____

What is my profit margin for each product?

_____

_____

Which should I try to sell more of and how?

_____

_____

Which products should I raise prices on, sell less, or stop selling altogether?

_____

_____

 Meditate **on these scriptures (***Sell*** more of your more profitable products):**

Focus on where you create the most value. Proverbs 31:18 (NIV): *"She sees that her trading is profitable."*

Lesson 4J: *Sell* on cash, not credit

 Follow expert advice (*Sell* on cash, not credit):

If at all possible, collect payment immediately when your customer receives your product. This will allow you to pay your bills and produce more products to sell to your next customers. (Remember the section on cash flow earlier in this module?) If they are accustomed to paying on credit (an account with you, not a credit card) you may want to offer them a 3-5% discount for paying right away. Consider whether your customer will be willing to pay a deposit in advance for large orders that require you to order expensive raw materials.

 Ask yourself (*Sell* on cash, not credit):

What are my customers' expectations on how and when they will pay?

_____

_____

Will I try a small discount to encourage more cash payments?

_____

_____

Will I seek advanced deposits from customers on large orders?

_____

_____

 Meditate on these scriptures (*Sell* on cash not credit):

Collecting right away strengthens your business to weather the unknown future. James 4:13-15 (NIV): *"Come now, you who say, "Today or tomorrow we will go into such and such a town and spend a year there and trade and make a profit"— yet you do not know what tomorrow will bring. What is your life? For you are a mist that appears for a little time and then vanishes. Instead you ought to say, "If the Lord wills, we will live and do this or that."*

Lesson 4K: *Pay* yourself a regular salary after your business is self-sustaining

 Follow expert advice (*Pay* yourself a regular salary after your business is self-sustaining):

Keep your personal and business money separate, with your salary being the only interaction between them. "When friends or family want you to use business funds to meet their needs, tell them you will be glad to share some of the milk (your salary), but not the cow (the business assets) since God entrusted the cow to produce milk for tomorrow too." (Al Steiner). This principle is well-illustrated by the diagrams below, which shows that your financial obligations to others should connect only to you (right), not to your business (left). This practice builds a healthy boundary around your business so that it can slowly gain the financial strength it will need to survive. Like a parent caring for an infant, you must take care of the baby now so it can take care of you later!

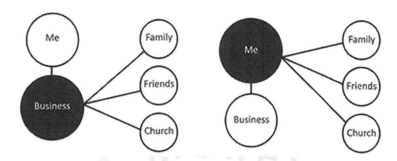

This graphic taken from Partners Worldwide's Business Curriculum for Small and Medium Enterprises, Copyright 2017, Used with permission.

In the beginning months (or years), you will need to pay your living expenses through another means so you can reinvest all (or most) of the revenue back into the business, but as soon as your cash flow can handle it, begin paying yourself a small regular salary and grow it over time as the business gains financial health.

 Ask yourself (*Pay* yourself a regular salary after your business is self-sustaining):

Do I keep my business money separate from my personal money?

_____

_____

Is my business self-sustaining or does it often have cash flow crises?

_____

_____

When might I be able to start or increase my salary?

_____

_____

How will I handle requests from family and friends?

_____

_____

 Meditate on these scriptures (*Pay yourself a regular salary after your business is self-sustaining*):

As your business is able, even a small paycheck can boost your morale. 1 Timothy 5:18 (ESV): *"For the Scripture says, 'You shall not muzzle an ox when it treads out the grain,' and, 'The laborer deserves his wages.'"*

Lesson 4L: *Give* 10% of your salary

 Follow expert advice (*Give* 10% of your salary):

The bible instructs you to give at least 10% of your income to God's work. This discipline helps you trust that God is your Provider. It loosens money's grip on your hearts and gives you the joy of generosity. "That joy comes from imitating God, from whom comes every good and perfect gift. He gave you Jesus Christ, and Jesus gave His life to give you life, so giving is one of the greatest ways to imitate Jesus and His Father. It's an act of worship that reminds you that all you have is a gift. Since God enables you to work, 100% of your salary is from Him. Giving back 10% is the starting point, but as God provides more income for you, consider increasing the percentage you give to the Lord's work." (Jeff Hostetter)

 Ask yourself (*Give* 10% of your salary):

Is fear or selfishness keeping me from giving?

What percentage of my salary am I giving now and what do I plan to increase it to?

_____

_____

Do I control money or does money control me?

_____

_____

Which of my mentors can share their experience in this area with me?

_____

_____

 Meditate on these (*Give* 10% of your salary):

God's stewards realize their money is not their own but is to be used for God's purposes. Psalm 37:21 (NIV): *"The wicked borrow and do not repay, but the righteous give generously."*

God blesses you so you can bless others. 2 Corinthians 9:6-11 (NIV): *'Remember this: Whoever sows sparingly will also reap sparingly, and whoever sows generously will also reap generously. Each of you should give what you have decided in your heart to give, not reluctantly or under compulsion, for God loves a cheerful giver. And God is able to bless you abundantly, so that in all things at all times, having all that you need, you will abound in every good work. As it is written: 'They have freely scattered their gifts to the poor; their righteousness endures forever.' Now He who supplies seed to the sower and bread for food will also supply and increase your store of seed and will enlarge the harvest of your righteousness. You will be enriched in every way so that you can be generous on every occasion, and through us your generosity will result in thanksgiving to God."*

 Observe teens who need advice:

Running into Maria's house, Alejandro triumphantly announced his news, "Okay, I have found a solution for us. You're going to love it!"

Maria wasn't so sure. After adding up all their expected costs, and then adding in even more for the unexpected ones, they had both felt completely overwhelmed. "Ok, I'm ready to hear the plan," she said rather unconvincingly.

"We can't afford rent, or an oven, or any of those things right now. Ok, I get it! But I talked to my aunt. She runs a catering business and she said, most weeks, she isn't using her kitchen during the week because the orders usually come in for big events on the weekend. So, if we will take care of everything, and clean it really well, and pay her 10% of what we make, we can use her kitchen! So, all we need to buy are the food supplies, then we make the tortillas and sell them!"

"Ok..." Maria responded slowly, thinking it through. "But, we need to figure out how many tortillas to make. And we need to budget for everything we'll need to transport them. But maybe this can work. I'm not sure, but let's run the numbers again – and then once more!" Alejandro really *was* a good negotiator! Plus, now they knew how much they would need to save to one day open their own store.

Avoid these top five mistakes:

1. Underestimating the costs of running your business.
2. Not keeping your personal and business finances separate.
3. Tying too much money up in inventory.
4. Competing on price instead of quality.
5. Not tracking expenses and analyzing trends.

Form these top five habits:

1. Save every week into a separate account. Start now even if it's a tiny amount, then increase as able.
2. Do as much as possible without loans and pay them off as quickly as possible.
3. Always know where all of your money is going.
4. Pay your employees first before other bills. Never miss a payday.
5. Keep working to speed up your cash flow.

Follow this real-life Honduran example:

When you first meet Suyapa Parafita with her long, straight hair, her kind eyes and warm hug will reveal the loving person she is. She'll likely ask you several questions to get to know you and show that she cares. Her other side is equally impressive: she's a veteran businesswoman who can make tough decisions and balance multiple businesses successfully. At the same time, she's a devoted wife, mother, church member, and business mentor. How does she do it all? She would say: "by the grace of God." Here are some ways she's lived out this module's expert advice about money. Here is how she explained it to Odile Perez.

Suyapa with her husband and son

Suyapa Parafita: *"We started Salud Natural to help promote healthier lifestyles to our fellow Hondurans by selling homeopathic remedies and supplements. Over the years, we learned how to correctly manage money in a business.*

One of the first money practices we started to implement was to save on a monthly basis for the extra salaries Honduran law requires we pay to our employees in June and December. To avoid the stress of not having the money available when it is due, we started to set aside a fixed amount each month. It was directly deposited into a separate account for that purpose. This helped us be reliable for our employees without all of the stress of scrambling for the money at the last minute.

When we found it necessary to take out our first business loan, we only borrowed what was really needed to buy inventory. That extra inventory generated enough money to pay back the loan on time, which opened the door to future loans. Speaking of inventory, to manage money properly, we have had to learn how to effectively track inventory. This is not an easy task. It can be overwhelming to track hundreds of products and frustrating since there aspects beyond our control. For example, on several occasions our orders from suppliers were delayed for weeks by customs. Our customers were not happy! We lost sales when we ran out of top selling items, while other times we had too much money tied up in inventory that was not selling. To avoid this, we began to order from our suppliers more frequently and focus on products in higher demand that sold faster.

A year ago we also began to check and analyze our cash flow statement and keep track of our biggest expenses. This is one of the best tools to see how were spending our money and how to better manage it. After closely reviewing our expenses, we realized that we needed to modify certain behaviors. For instance, we started to lower the extra incentives we were offering our customers and redirect this money to pay off our inventory.

We also began calculating the profit margin of each product. Based on the margins, we determined whether or not to sell a product or to have more of another. Our business greatly benefited as we stopped selling products with low margins and weak demand, and began offering products with higher margins and stronger demand. Moreover, we never started a war on prices. Instead, we let our high quality of service and products satisfy our customers to the point that they were willing to pay the price.

Lastly, we have learned to incentivize customers to pay us immediately with cash rather than buying on credit. By offering a small discount for cash purchases, we dramatically increased our cash flow. This reduced our stress as we were able to pay our bills on time and replenish our inventory.

As a company we have come a long way in how we manage our money, yet we understand the need to continue to grow in this area, as it is the best way to ensure the longevity and sustainability of our business."

Notice that in Suyapa's business, all of the parts of this module's expert advice are intricately connected. In a real-life business, they are not separate, unrelated lessons. Rather, savings, loans, inventory, tracking margins and cash flow all work hand-in-hand. A weakness in one area can wreak havoc on the other areas. On the other hand, following best practices in each area builds strength in the others.

 Do with your group:

Susana sells pupusas in the El Centro market. After reading *Start*Book, she wants to make her grandmother's pupusa recipe with the highest level of excellence and sell them at a profitable price. What are some things that would make customers feel good about paying 10% more than her nearby competitors charge?

Teacher's guide: Possible answers include: friendly service, better ingredients, more variety, food that's fresh, hot, delivered and protected from insects, better packaging, condiments and napkins available.

 Apply this module with:

PRAYER – Ask God how much I should give to his work. Pray about how to handle it when friends or family ask for money from my business.

RESEARCH – Look into loan options and rates. Find out what competitors are charging for products similar to mine and if they sell them on credit.

CREATIVITY – Write a savings plan, including how much to save weekly for what purpose.

ACTION – Open a business savings account and consider joining a savings association.

CUSTOMERS – Ask potential customers whether they expect to pay on credit and whether they would make a deposit for large orders.

MENTORS – Get help as needed with the above calculations. Ask about their experience in learning to tithe.

MONEY – Separate my business finances from my personal finances. Start saving a portion from the business finances each week. Estimate when and how much to start paying myself. Give more than usual to God's work this week and ponder how it affects my heart. Estimate costs by category for my launch and my ongoing business operations. Add up all business expenses for last month and identify my top five expense categories. Add the number of units sold for each product in a month and then decide how much raw materials to order how often. Calculate my breakeven point and profit margin for each product, then consider whether I should decrease my production costs, raise my prices, or sell more or less of certain products.

TIME – Estimate how long it will take to save up my costs to launch. Set aside a time each day to track my ongoing expenses. Set aside time each month to calculate my top five expenses and go over it with my mentor.

 Practice values of Compassion International:

Integrity – Everyone wants to do business with people who keep their promises. The possibility of attracting more customers encourages entrepreneurs to live with integrity. Cheating others gives short-term gains, but long-term success comes by building trust.

Excellence – Profitability is the simplest measure of the value you're creating for your customers. The same goes for whether your customers gladly pay you a higher price (as you do at a fancy restaurant as opposed to fast food).

Stewardship – Saving, giving, and efficiently using money is the proper response to the fact that everything belongs to God and He trusts us to be responsible with it.

Dignity – God's creation continues to pour out blessings year after year, so building businesses that continue to create wealth remind us of our dignity as the only creatures who share the Creator's image.

 Evaluate the teen business:

Alejandro and Maria have found a creative solution to minimize the cost of starting their business. Finding ways to *not* spend money is an important lesson for entrepreneurs.

Imagine that Alejandro and Maria came to you and asked for a loan. They plan to use your money to buy what they need to market their business, create tortillas, and deliver them. What questions would you ask them before agreeing to loan them money?

- How much money do you think they will need to get started?
- How much money do you think they can make each week?
- How long will it take them to pay back your loan with interest?

Sum it up:

Money is exciting but tracking numbers on a page isn't. If you don't learn to analyze your money, you're flying blind and your business will suffer. Get help from one of your mentors to master this discipline. It will certainly pay off! Make good money plans and stick to them. You'll be glad you did as profitable businesses do not magically appear. Rather, they grow through disciplined effort over time. You are God's steward over the resources he's entrusted to you and he expects you to multiply them to provide for the needs of your family and community.

Use your *Start*Book Plan:

Now that you've completed this module, please fill out your *Start*Book Plan on the next page. Think about what you've learned and choose the most important goal for you to apply this module to your business over the next 12 months. Write down your goal, three actions to accomplish it, and dates to complete each one. Refer to your *Start*Book Plan often as a tool to grow your business.

StartBook Plan

4. Money

Module snapshot: There's never enough money for everything, so you must direct it toward your priorities. Diligently follow these best practices to control your money and patiently build wealth.

My #1 "Money" goal for the next 12 months:

My top 3 action steps to accomplish this goal:

1.

Today's date: _____ Target completion date: _____ Actual completion date: _____

2.

Today's date: _____ Target completion date: _____ Actual compl 'ion date: _____

3.

Today's date: _____ Target completion date: _____ Actual completion date: _____

5. Launch

Module snapshot: Give attention to these important details to plan a successful launch.

Module 5: LAUNCH

Consider module snapshot: Give attention to these important details to plan a successful launch.

Observe teens who need advice:

After reviewing their finances one Saturday, Alejandro started talking excitedly, "Well Maria, it took us two months of doing all the work we could find, and saving every lempira we could, but wow! Now we have the money. Time to go!"

Maria smiled. Alejandro's eternal optimism had kept them motivated while they had prepared for this day. She couldn't help but feel happy. "It is good! And after working so hard to save this money, I think we will be very careful with it now. Let's review our launch plan again."

Alejandro went over the details. "Ok, we've got our menu. Four of the most delicious tortillas you could ever want. At my birthday party last week, everyone said they were the best they'd ever had! Now, we know students at the university are always hungry. So, here's the plan: we take pictures of our amazing food, put posters all around campus, and spread the word: "get lunch delivered!" They message us what they want, you make it, I deliver it, then we clean up together. I can't wait!"

A week later, Alejandro and Maria looked at one another in

desperation. "We have a problem, Alejandro! We have a hundred orders for tortillas, but I only bought supplies for fifty. Besides, you can't deliver a hundred in time! What are we going to do?"

Lesson 5A: *Find* a smart location

 Follow expert advice (*Find* a smart location):

If selling in a location which is visible and convenient to your customers is important, then consider that when choosing a location. If such a space (corner store, mall kiosk) is expensive and small, decide whether it makes sense for you to produce your products in a different place than where you sell them. For services such as house cleaning or plumbing, you work at your customers' locations but will need a place to store your tools. Make a list of needs and a list of wants regarding your location(s).

You may not be able to afford starting in your ideal location. Start small to learn if you're sales will support a place with higher rent. Perhaps a family member or friend has a location you can use at a discounted rate for a period of time. Pay them at least a small amount (so that it is a dignified transaction, not a handout) and put the rental agreement in writing.

Install a sign where you sell your products. Have your sign up the *very first day* you sell at that location. Make your logo and tagline as large as possible so passersby will instantly know what you can do for them. Do not include your phone number so you do not attract the wrong kind of attention.

 Ask yourself (*Find* a smart location):

Will I produce and sell in the same or different spaces?

_____

_____

Can I use my home initially for one or both?

_____

_____

On my location wish list, which attributes are *needs* and which are *wants?*

_____

_____

Do I have friends or family with a location I can use at little cost?

_____

_____

Can I trade my products for at least part of the rent?

_____

_____

Is my top choice of location convenient for my best customers?

_____

_____

Is it visible enough to attract new customers?

_____

_____

What will be the size, location, colors and contents of my sign?

_____

_____

Who will produce it and when?

_____

_____

How much do I need to save up so my sign is ready on opening day?

_____

_____

What precautions will I take to secure the property and avoid unwanted attention?

_____

_____

 Meditate **on these scriptures (*Find* a smart location):**

A location close to your customers puts them first. Philippians 2:3-4 (NIV): *"Do nothing out of selfish ambition or vain conceit. Rather, in humility value others above yourselves, not looking to your own interests but each of you to the interests of the others."*

Lesson 5B: *Acquire* the right tools

 Follow your expert (*Acquire* the right tools):

While you may not be able to afford the best tools and equipment right away, you need to have the bare minimum. You may have to do some work by hand that a machine could do much faster. "Handmade" might even be a selling point that is attractive to your customers! This is an area where your God-given creativity must come in. What equipment can you borrow, rent, make yourself, or trade something you have for? Don't let this issue cripple you; with enough heart and hustle you'll find a way to get better and better tools over time until you have the best available. Set goals for when you plan to save enough to acquire better tools.

 Ask yourself (*Acquire* the right tools):

What is the minimum amount of equipment I'll need to launch my business and how can I creatively acquire them with limited funds?

Who believes in me and can help me brainstorm solutions to this need?

_____

_____

What is my plan and timeline to move from basic tools to the best available?

_____

_____

 Meditate on these scriptures (*Acquire* the right tools):

Properly maintained tools can increase your efficiency. Ecclesiastes 10:10 (ESV): *"If the iron is blunt, and one does not sharpen the edge, he must use more strength, but wisdom helps one to succeed."*

Lesson 5C: *Comply* with government requirements

 Follow expert advice (*Comply* with government requirements):

Learn what registrations, regulations, and taxes you will need to comply with. While a small hobby doesn't require government registration, find out the level of revenue at which you're required to formalize your business (50,000 lempiras in Honduras). Ask an established entrepreneur or attorney you know to show you the ropes. While complying with government taxes and fees reduces your profit, it honors God and communicates to potential customers that you are a legitimate business.

 Ask yourself (*Comply* with government requirements):

Who can help me learn what my local government requirements are and how to follow them?

_____

_____

Do I believe that God will bless me as I obey him?

_____

_____

Do I trust God to take care of me when taxes threaten to cripple my business?

_____

_____

If I cheat on my taxes, what other shortcuts might I be tempted to take?

_____

_____

Who can I be a good example to in this area?

_____

_____

Meditate on these scriptures (*Comply* with government requirements):

Following the law reflects our submission to God. Romans 13:1 (ESV): *"Let every person be subject to the governing authorities."*

Government has legitimate – but not ultimate - claims on you. Matthew 22:19-21 (NIV): *"Show me the coin used for paying the tax." They brought him a denarius, and he asked them, "Whose image is this? And whose inscription?" "Caesar's," they replied. Then he said to them, "So give back to Caesar what is Caesar's, and to God what is God's."*

Lesson 5D: *Open* your business bank accounts

 Follow expert advice (*Open* your business bank accounts):

At a local community bank which offers small business loans in your industry, open your business checking and savings accounts (see Lesson 4A on saving money). Hopefully, this is a bank where you've already established a good banking history through your personal checking account. Whenever you write a check, balance your checking account ledger right away so you never write a bad check – which is expensive in fees and broken trust. The bank's loan officer will check your banking history if you ever apply for a loan.

 Ask yourself (***Open*** your business bank accounts):

Which bank is most likely to loan money to my business in the future, if needed?

_____

_____

Do I have a good history at my current personal bank or should I make a fresh start elsewhere?

_____

_____

What bank do my parents and mentors advise I use?

_____

_____

Do I need to learn to balance a checkbook?

_____

_____

When will I open my business checking and savings accounts?

_____

_____

 Meditate on these scriptures (*Open* your business bank accounts):

Using a bank helps you protect, mobilize, and track your resources. 1 Corinthians 14:33 (NIV): *"For God is not a God of disorder but of peace—as in all the congregations of the Lord's people."*

Lesson 5E: *Protect* your business through insurance

 Follow expert advice (*Protect* your business through insurance):

Business insurance types for small businesses include general liability and commercial auto. These will reimburse you for losses due to theft, flood, fire or accident. Discuss with a mentor or insurance agent which types of insurance and how much coverage you need at this point in your business. The more you have to lose, the more important it is for you to have insurance.

Those who don't buy insurance when they launch often put it off until it is too late as you'll read in this module's case study. The cost of insurance is small compared to the benefit it offers. Even if you never have to use it, it offers peace of mind that your years of investment will not be destroyed in a moment.

Insurance is not unlimited, but rather expects you to take necessary precautions against losses. If the loss results from your negligence, insurance will probably not honor your claim. So be wise.

God is your Provider, so He alone is worthy of your ultimate trust. However, insurance is one of the good things He provides through business. It may be one of the ways He want to provide for you.

 Ask yourself (***Protect*** your business through insurance):

What are the biggest things that could go wrong in my business and is there a type of insurance that could cover that loss?

_____

_____

Which of my mentors can teach me about insurance and refer a trustworthy insurance agent to me?

_____

_____

What precautions can I take against losses?

_____

_____

When and how much insurance will I need?

_____

_____

 ***Meditate* on these scriptures (*Protect* your business through insurance):**

Sound discretion leads to security. Proverbs 3:21-26 (NIV): *"My son, do not let wisdom and understanding out of your sight, preserve sound judgment and discretion; they will be life for you, an ornament to grace your neck.*

Then you will go on your way in safety, and your foot will not stumble. When you lie down, you will not be afraid; when you lie down, your sleep will be sweet. Have no fear of sudden disaster or of the ruin that overtakes the wicked, for the LORD will be at your side and will keep your foot from being snared."

Lesson 5F: *Get* feedback through a soft launch

Follow expert advice (*Get* feedback through a soft launch):

Before your grand opening to the public, host a soft launch with family, friends and mentors. Persistently ask for critical feedback so you can improve your products and the way you deliver them. If you sell from a physical location, get feedback on your layout, décor, product packaging and displays, then make the necessary improvements between your soft launch and grand opening. Do the same with your website and Facebook page.

Ask yourself (*Get* feedback through a soft launch):

Who will I invite to my soft launch?

_____

_____

What questions will I ask to get their honest, even critical, feedback?

_____

_____

When will my soft launch be?

_____

_____

What preparations do I need to make?

_____

_____

 Meditate on these scriptures (*Get* feedback through a soft launch):

People who care about you can help you see your blind spots. Proverbs 15:22 (NIV): *"Plans fail for lack of counsel, but with many advisers they succeed."*

Lesson 5G: *Publicize* a grand opening

 Follow expert advice (*Publicize* a grand opening):

Start with a bang! Get the word out every way you can and have specials (door prizes or samples or discounts) to draw people in. Have special decorations and make a great first impression with your friendliness and excellence. If possible, get contact information from your first customers so you can alert them of specials and new products or services in the future. Have your mentors, family and friends come out to support you as well. Provide marketing materials for attendees to take home to learn more about your business. "Grand" doesn't mean "perfect", since your skills, equipment, and location will be a work-in-progress for a while. Delaying launch for too long is usually due to fear masked by various excuses. Rise up to the challenge; the Lord is with you!

 Ask yourself (*Publicize* a grand opening):

What are all the ways I can publicize my grand opening?

_____

_____

What do I want my customers to experience?

_____

_____

What specials will I create to draw a crowd?

_____

_____

How will I decorate the location?

_____

_____

When will I have my grand opening and what fears might tempt me to delay it for too long?

_____

_____

What marketing materials will I hand out?

_____

_____

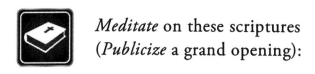

Meditate on these scriptures
(*Publicize* a grand opening):

The work of preparing and promoting your launch is worthwhile. Proverbs 14:23 (NIV): *"All hard work brings a profit, but mere talk leads only to poverty."*

Observe teens who follow advice:

Two weeks later, Alejandro and Maria sat down to review the state of their business. It had cost a lot of money to print a second round of posters, but they had to raise their prices so they could hire two more people to help with deliveries during lunch time – and to help clean the kitchen before Alejandro's aunt needed it. Still, Mario and his brother were grateful for the work!

Also, dozens of people had been frustrated that they couldn't get a "dream" tortilla the first week. But then, Alejandro and Maria were surprised that this had only increased the students' desire to try again the next day – and the next! After sharing their problem with a mentor, their posters now proudly said, "Only serving the first two hundred customers a day – chase 'the dream' while you can!" The unexpected scarcity of their delicious tortillas let them sell out every day — and they could plan exactly how much food to buy in the mornings.

"So Alejandro, you were right –this is going great!" said Maria. "I never thought we'd sell out every day. And we've even hired Mario. But what's next? It is exciting to see everyone talking about our food, but I don't know how we're going to be ready to sell more than two hundred tortillas a day!"

Avoid these top five mistakes:

1. Starting with a location you can't afford.
2. Not registering your business with the government.
3. Spending too much on your grand opening.
4. Not installing a sign that is big enough, clear enough, and professional enough to attract new customers.
5. Not protecting your business with insurance.

Form these top five habits:

1. Continually upgrade your tools until you have the best.
2. Build caring relationships with your customers.
3. Pay your taxes.
4. Keep working towards earning credentials that will build trust with customers.
5. Meet regularly with a bank loan officer.

Follow this real-life Honduran example:

Hector's four daughters are blessed because he is the dad that many only wish they had. Hector David Euceda is a big guy, but he's safe – more likely to shed a tear than throw a punch. His wide smile doesn't show his teeth, but does show he's both kind and reserved. That smile nearly shuts his eyes, but you can't miss his rugged eyebrows which peak like mountains. His big heart is also ever-apparent – in the way he rehabilitates troubled employees and dreams about building drug rehabilitation centers with his business profits. When he heard about our Haitian friend Cereste whose bakery roof was destroyed in the 2010 earthquake, he immediately took $200 US out of his wallet to get it rebuilt. So generous! Hector even plans to create 2,000 jobs to bless his country. He's pretty ambitious, yet humble at the same time as you'll see in the mistakes he admits to below. In fact, you'll mostly learn in this story the danger of <u>not</u> following this module's expert advice! Here's what Hector shared with Odile Pérez.

Hector & Telma's furniture manufacturing plant burned to the ground on October 27, 2015

The aftermath

Hector with his wife and daughter in front of furniture they manufacture.

Hector Euceda: *"My wife (Telma Muñoz Colindres) and I opened a furniture business we named Muebles Ripressa in January 2005 with just $5,000 Lempiras and one machine in our one employee's home. We started with no capital, but with a great dream to create many jobs for our country. Ten years later, we had built up to 45 loyal customers who bought $1 million Lempiras worth of furniture every month. Yet despite our growth and prosperity, things were not being done correctly. This became clear on October 27th, 2015 when a blazing fire wiped out everything in our factory. It was caused by an electrical problem at a business that was in the same building as ours. Thankfully, there was no one in the building since we had closed early that day. When I heard the news, I breathed this prayer: 'God you know why you do things. Please give me wisdom and your strength to handle this situation.' When I got to the warehouse and saw it in flames, I felt worried and sad to see our years of work going up in flames. But praise to God, I still felt a sense of calmness and peace.*

I had taken on a lot of unnecessary debt, owing 50% more than our assets. Our factory burnt down, but our debts didn't. This tragedy exposed our reality; we were doing things by inertia and financial ignorance. Although we had received advice from Creating Jobs Inc, we didn't apply enough of it. One of our biggest mistakes was that in 2015 we failed to pay our business insurance as it didn't seem important, leaving us vulnerable when the unthinkable happened: a $4 million Lempira loss!"

Evan notes that just as Hector helped the Haitian baker rebuild, he now received help from his church family, Creating Jobs Inc, and others to rebuild his own business. "Give and you will receive" as Jesus said in Luke 6:38 (NLT).

Hector continues: *"This time, we were determined to launch the right way by meeting all of the government's requirements and by seeking wisdom from a business mentor* (Saul Contrares whose story is told in module 2) *in our church. A big step was to find the right location, especially one with a low risk of fire. Here are some precautions we've taken: we have our own transformers, and our electrical wiring was done by professionals to prevent another short circuit. Each work area has its own fire extinguisher, and is close to an emergency exit. Also, now we don't share our warehouse with another business, so we won't suffer from their mistakes.*

We also made sure our new location was affordable, accessible to customers, and big enough for our production, office, and showroom needs. It is much bigger, yet half the price of the one that burnt down. Next, we invested $250,000 Lempiras in tools, including five machines that help us produce 500 furniture pieces at once. We hired just enough people with the right technical expertise: carpenters, cabinetmakers, sanders, painters, and craftsmen. We worked smartly but also quickly, relaunching only a month after the fire. We called our 12 main customers to say 'we're back in business.'

We've finally learned to correctly manage our finances and protect our business with vigilance. We understand that we must manage risks since challenges and mishaps are inevitable, so we're careful to pay our insurance on time! Although we are now more cautious when making decisions, our vision continues to give us strength as we keep dreaming of those 2,000 jobs that we will create. Success is falling then getting up and moving forward, but relying on God to do so."

Life dishes out "reality checks" in our broken world, which can either break you or make you wiser. Hector and Telma were certainly more cautious in getting the details right for their relaunch, but their big dreams never went up in smoke. By God's grace, you too can be careful in planning your launch while dreaming big dreams of what He can do through you.

Do with your group:

Split class into three groups to rank these factors in choosing a location to sell their products, with one being "most important" and seven being "least important": affordable price, highly visible, close to customer, close to entrepreneur's home, trustworthy landlord, large enough space, and attractive building. Have groups share their rankings with the whole group and explain their reasons.

Teacher's guide: Provide pen and paper and have each group designate someone to write and present their rankings.

 Apply this module with:

PRAYER – Pray about when to formalize my business and for help to trust God to provide despite unreasonably high taxes. Pray about when I am ready to launch (There comes a point where more preparation is less valuable than the learning gained by actually running a business.)

RESEARCH – Find location options for production and sales.

CREATIVITY – Write down size, placement, contents, colors and type of sign for my location. Make a list of friends, family, and mentors to invite to my soft launch.

ACTION – Open my business checking account. Get quotes from two sign companies. Explore banks that meet my needs. Find out types of insurance I need and get quotes from two agents. Plan, prep, and host my grand opening.

CUSTOMERS – Promote my grand opening to a large number of potential customers.

MENTORS – Discuss what equipment I'll need and how to get it. Get help navigating government regulations.

MONEY – Balance my checkbook daily. Create a launch budget, with estimated amounts for location, tools, skills training, employee pay, government fees, opening bank balances, insurance, and grand opening.

TIME – Since I have more time than money at the beginning, consider which launch efforts I can do myself rather than paying suppliers for.

 ## *Practice* values of Compassion International:

Integrity – Complying with government requirements demonstrates your obedience to the Bible. Living out who you claim to be is the definition of integrity.

Excellence – Acquiring the best tools help you do your best work, which mimics God's "very good" work.

Stewardship – Protecting your business through insurance honors God's investment in your talents and your responsibility to provide for your family and employees.

Dignity – If your family helps your launch with a location or some equipment, paying them something for it over time reinforces that you are one who creates – not consumes – value.

Evaluate the teen business:

Imagine that Alejandro and Maria came to you for advice. Review the advice in this module. Then, answer these two questions:

1. What have they done well so far? What is going well with the launch of their business? How would you encourage them?
2. What important steps have they overlooked so far? What actions and habits would you advise them to pay attention to before they think about expanding their business?

Sum it up:

Launching a rocket into space requires both mundane and exciting milestones that take time and discipline. The same holds true for your business. While you'll enjoy some of these steps more than others, each will set you up for success. Godspeed to you!

Use your *Start*Book Plan:

Now that you've completed this module, please fill out your *Start*Book Plan on the next page. Think about what you've learned and choose the most important goal for you to apply this module to your business over the next 12 months. Write down your goal, three actions to accomplish it, and dates to complete each one. Refer to your *Start*Book Plan often as a tool to grow your business.

StartBook Plan

5. Launch

Module snapshot: Give attention to these important details to plan a successful launch.

My #1 "Launch" goal for the next 12 months:

My top 3 action steps to accomplish this goal:

1.

Today's date: _____ Target completion date: _____ Actual completion date: _____

2.

Today's date: _____ Target completion date: _____ Actual completion date: _____

3.

Today's date: _____ Target completion date: _____ Actual completion date: _____

6. Customers

Module snapshot: Identify your ideal customers and find the right message and means to reach them. Make them so happy that they bring their friends to you.

Module 6: CUSTOMERS

Consider module snapshot: Identify your ideal customers and find the right message and means to reach them. Make them so happy that they bring their friends to you.

Observe teens who need advice:

A month later, Maria was shocked to see so few messages on her phone. "Alejandro, we need to talk!" she shouted. The orders for lunch were down. Only 156 tortillas. Usually there were well over 200 requests.

After hearing the disappointing update, Alejandro offered his bright smile. "I have an idea! When we deliver the tortillas today, we'll ask everyone what's going on at the school, and if they have any ideas for us. I'll be back soon! We can handle one bad day, right?"

Maria sighed. "Ok, I'm counting on you! We need to figure this out. And you can count on me to make the best tortillas *ever* today!"

Lesson 6A: Identify your ideal customers

 Follow expert advice (Identify your ideal customers):

Instead of trying to sell to everyone, find out what type of person is most likely to be excited about your products. Find out their age, sex, marital status, income, occupation and interests. They may not be an individual at all. If you sell to businesses that use or resell your products, learn which size and types of businesses need your solution.

An important part of identifying your ideal customers is their location. The most profitable sales are the ones near you, since customers buy what they need close to home and you'd be silly to ship your cookies to another country if you can sell them all here. Of course, online delivery of software products makes worldwide delivery feasible. So, decide how big the geography of your market should be.

If you try to sell to everyone, you–may end up selling to no one. "An army everywhere is an army nowhere" (Tzu, 2017). So focus.

Ask yourself (*Identify* your ideal customers):

What type of person or business has shown the most interest in my product or service?

_____

_____

Are there enough of them to sustain my business?

_____

_____

What is the geographic limit of who I hope to sell to?

_____

_____

 Meditate on these scriptures (*Identify* your ideal customers):

Wisely assess who you're dealing with. Luke 14:31-32 (NIV): *"Or suppose a king is about to go to war against another king. Won't he first sit down and consider whether he is able with ten thousand*

men to oppose the one coming against him with twenty thousand? If he is not able, he will send a delegation while the other is still a long way off and will ask for terms of peace."

Lesson 6B: *Write* marketing messages about your solution

Follow expert advice (*Write* marketing messages about your solution):

After you identify the type and location of your best customers, you can better shape your marketing messages to reach them. A flier to share about your business with an urban teen would be different than one for a countryside farmer. Speak their language. "Make them feel you are speaking to them personally." (Lee Murray) Show how your products solve your ideal customers' problems and meet their needs.

Your marketing message has two parts: "headline" and "body". The headline is the most important because customers decide from the headline whether they will take the time to read the body. Make it short, unexpected and about your audience. A headline in the form of a question can get them thinking. Don't try to say everything – just spark their curiosity to keep reading. Write lots of possible headlines, then choose your top five to get feedback from customers, parents and mentors.

Just below your headline, the body should expound on the headline and show the value your product or service can give to them. Try to reach them on an emotional level since our brains make decisions on emotion more than reason. Use a story – about them – if possible. Recall how most commercials use a storyline.

 Ask yourself (*Write* marketing messages about your solution):

What kind of message would best reach my ideal customers?

_____

_____

What storyline connects them to my solution?

_____

_____

What are five possible headlines I could use?

_____

_____

Which of them do my mentors, parents, and customers say is the best?

_____

_____

What should I focus on in the body of my marketing message?
_____

_____

Do my headline and body go well together?

_____

_____

 Meditate on these scriptures (*Write* marketing messages about your solution):

It takes effort to focus on what you can do for others rather than saying whatever comes to mind. Proverbs 18:2(ESV): *"A fool takes no pleasure in understanding, but only in expressing his opinion."*

Lesson 6C: *Print* your marketing materials

 Follow expert advice (*Print* your marketing materials):

Find out what kinds of marketing materials your ideal customers use to find products like yours. You may want to print a small amount of these to see if they are effective: business cards, fliers, brochures, product packaging and signs. Include your logo and tagline on each. Make sure the color scheme of your graphics fits with your logo. Print all the materials in the same style so it's obvious that they go together. Of course, you'll need to adjust the length of the body of your marketing message to fit the different formats.

 Ask yourself (*Print* your marketing materials):

Which types of materials will reach my ideal customers?

_____

_____

Do my mentors have a print shop to recommend?

_____

_____

What color scheme goes with my logo?

_____

_____

What graphics go with my marketing message?

_____

_____

What is my budget for this?

_____

_____

 Meditate on these scriptures (_Print_ your marketing materials):

Invest in connecting with your customers and you'll be rewarded. 2 Corinthians 9:6 (ESV): _"Whoever sows sparingly will reap sparingly, but he who sows bountifully will reap bountifully."_

Lesson 6D: *Build* your marketing channels

 Follow expert advice (*Build* your marketing channels):

Find out where your ideal customers search for your products, then build a presence there. This might include a website, Facebook page and ads, Twitter, and YouTube channel. Learn to use these effectively to educate and attract your customers. Keep them up to date and always have a "call to action" for them to engage with you. If you build trust by educating them about their problem and your solution, they'll be more likely to buy from you. Learn about "search engine optimization" and use the latest techniques to improve your Google rankings.

 Ask yourself (*Build* your marketing channels):

Will I build a website myself using free or inexpensive tools or can I afford to pay a web designer to build it for me?

Does the person building the site know how to improve Google rankings?

_____

_____

Will I sell online or use the website to encourage them to connect with me in person?

_____

_____

What valuable information can I provide online that will build my credibility as an expert in my industry?

_____

_____

What social media channels do my ideal customers use?

_____

_____

What are my plans to build a presence there?

_____

_____

Meditate on these scriptures (*Build* your marketing channels):

Spread your net wide for a bigger catch. Luke 5:4 (NIV): *"When He had finished speaking, He said to Simon, "Put out into the deep water and let down your nets for a catch."*

Lesson 6E: *Go* see your ideal customers in person

 Follow expert advice (*Go* see your ideal customers in person):

Don't wait for clients to find you. Instead, block out large chunks of time each week to go to them in person. "Face-to-face is the most personal way to build trust and bring their attention to the uniqueness of your product and a free sample or demonstration of it" (Lee Murray). Since a steady stream of new customers is your biggest need, spend the majority of your time and creative energy on finding them and making them extremely happy. Fear keeps many new entrepreneurs from doing this. Do the hard thing and it will become easier over time. Be courageous and don't let distractions and excuses keep you from doing what will grow your business. Remember from Lesson 1G the difference between urgent and important uses of time? This is both! You need to find more new customers to replace those who leave for whatever reason. Beware of relying too much on a few customers.

 Ask yourself (*Go* see your ideal customers in person):

If my top three customers died today, would my business survive?

_____

_____

Do I have all the customers I need and want?

_____

_____

If not, is there anything that should be a higher priority?

_____

_____

How many hours per week can I block off for this?

_____

_____

Which days of the week are best for my customers?

_____

_____

What fears and distractions might keep me from following through on this plan?

_____

_____

Who can keep me accountable to stick to my plan?

_____

_____

 Meditate on these scriptures (*Go* see your ideal customers in person):

Doing hard things takes courage and brings growth. Joshua 1:9 (NIV): *"Have I not commanded you? Be strong and courageous. Do not be afraid; do not be discouraged, for the LORD your God will be with you wherever you go."*

There is always an excuse to take the easy route. Ecclesiastes 11:4 *"He who observes the wind will not sow, and he who regards the clouds will not reap."*

Lesson 6F: *Explore* several sales and delivery channels

 Follow expert advice (*Explore* several sales and delivery channels):

Different ways of making sales include: door-to-door, phone, website, Ebay, Etsy, Amazon, app, retail store, outdoor market, and kiosk. You naturally gravitate towards one particular channel, but at least consider whether there is a great opportunity for you in a second or third channel. For some businesses, delivery is separate from sales. Different ways of getting your product to customers include: kiosk, retail store, personal delivery, shipping company, and online download. It would be great if more than one are possible, customers love options.

 Ask yourself (*Explore* several sales and delivery channels):

Where does my ideal customer want to buy and receive my product?

Which of the above sales and delivery channels should I consider?

_____

_____

Who can I get help from for channels that I'm not familiar with?

_____

_____

Which delivery channels are least expensive for me?

_____

_____

Which will I make possible (at different price points) for my customers?

_____

_____

 Meditate **on these scriptures (***Explore*** several sales and delivery channels):**

Relentlessly exploring where to sell brings ample provision. 2 Thessalonians 3:7-8 (NIV): *"For you yourselves know how you ought to follow our example. We were not idle when we were with you, nor did we eat anyone's food without paying for it. On the contrary, we*

worked night and day, laboring and toiling so that we would not be a burden to any of you."

Lesson 6G: *Grow* your sales

 Follow expert advice (*Grow* your sales):

Refer to your monthly fixed costs (Lesson 4F) and profit margin (Lesson 4I) to see how many sales you need to cover your expenses. For example, if you sell 1,000 products for $11/each this month, you'll generate $11,000 in revenue. If your fixed and variable costs add up to $10,000 for the month, that $1,000 above your breakeven point is your profit, giving you a 9% profit margin (1,000/11,000=.09). Is that $1,000 enough to pay your salary and meet your monthly savings goal (Lesson 4A)? If not, how far short does it fall? If it's $90 short, you'll need to sell another $1,000 worth (91 products) next month to cover your costs, salary, and savings. Based on the sum of these three items, set sales goals for each month and try to exceed what you sold during the same month last year. To increase sales, you'll need determination (Lesson 1C), more time with ideal customers (Lesson 6E), and the sales techniques we'll share later in this module.

Ask yourself (*Grow* your sales)

Are my monthly sales totals going up or down and why?

_____

_____

Are my sales currently covering all my fixed costs?

_____

_____

Are they also funding my savings and salary goals?

_____

_____

What is my monthly revenue from sales on average this year?

_____

_____

What do I want it to be next year?

_____

_____

What actions will I take to increase sales to reach my goals?

_____

_____

 Meditate on these scriptures (*Grow your sales*):

If you're not moving forward, you're moving backwards. Proverbs 18:9 (NIV): *"One who is slack in his work is brother to one who destroys."*

Lesson 6H: *Encourage* existing customers to buy more often

 Follow expert advice (*Encourage* existing customers to buy more often):

Your best source of new sales is from people who already buy from you. Leverage that trust (assuming they had a good experience the first time!) by encouraging them to buy from you again. You can have a frequent buyer's reward program where they get a free product after 10 purchases. Or you can make a schedule where you're calling them to remind them to come back after a certain period of time (three weeks for a haircut, three months for an oil change, six months for teeth cleaning, etc.). If you offer a service (water purification, tire rotation, or pressure washing), let them know after the first sale that you'll come back to give a free inspection in six months. This will give you an opportunity to give further recommendations that may lead to a sale.

 Ask yourself (*Encourage* existing customers to buy more often):

How will I remind past customers that I'm here to solve their problem again?

_____

_____

How often will I invite them to come back for more?

_____

_____

Meditate on these scriptures (*Grow your sales*):

Making customers happy will bring them back. Luke 6:38 (NIV): "Give, and it will be given to you. A good measure, pressed down, shaken together and running over, will be poured into your lap. For with the measure you use, it will be measured to you."

Lesson 61: *Invite* customers to buy more during each visit

 Follow expert advice (*Invite* customers to buy more during each visit):

It takes a lot of work to gain a new customer, so don't forget to offer more solutions to customers you already have. Ask customers who buy one of your products to try your other products and services. Do this gently and tastefully. You can let them know about your other products in a variety of ways: signs in your store, a 5% discount for trying another one of your products, mentioning it personally, announcing new products through your email newsletter or Facebook page.

Ask yourself (*Invite* customers to buy more during each visit):

Do I have more than one product or service?

_____

_____

Is there a product I could add that fits well with my business (using the same location, tools, and employees)?

_____

_____

How will I let customers know about my other products and services?

_____

_____

How will I tastefully and gently ask them to buy more?

_____

_____

Meditate on these scriptures (*Invite* customers to buy more during each visit):

Provide as much value to customers as possible while you are with them. Ephesians 5:15-16 (NIV): *"Be very careful, then, how you live—not as unwise but as wise, making the most of every opportunity..."*

Lesson 6J: *Provide* extraordinary customer service

 Follow expert advice (*Provide* extraordinary customer service):

The communication before, during and after the sale is as important as the sale itself! People are relational beings, so they need and want friendly and attentive interactions with you. They're buying the experience as much as the product. Ask for, then act on their feedback to improve your products.

Ask yourself (*Provide* extraordinary customer service):

Am I treating customers as humans or just as buyers?

_____

_____

Do I enjoy my interactions with them or do I see them as distractions from my "real" work?

_____

_____

Do I consistently smile and say "thank you"?

_____

_____

Do I follow up after the sale to see how their experience was?

_____

_____

Do I take action on their feedback?

_____

_____

Meditate on these scriptures (*Provide* extraordinary customer service):

Imitate Jesus' excellence. Mark 7:37 (NIV): *"People were overwhelmed with amazement. 'He has done everything well,' they said. 'He even makes the deaf hear and the mute speak.'"*

Lesson 6K: *Be* reliable

 Follow expert advice (*Be* reliable):

Consistently provide customers with more than they expect to earn their trust. Don't compromise on the quality of your product, delivering it on time and right the first time. "Provide the best solution every single time" (Lee Murray). They will buy again and bring their friends. Remember how important your character is to the success of your business?

Ask yourself (*Be* reliable):

Am I living out my marketing message or is it just hype?

_____

_____

Would I be embarrassed if my customers saw or heard me when I'm making my products?

_____

_____

Am I truly offering superior products?

_____

_____

 Meditate on these scriptures (*Be* Reliable):

Keeping your promises will build a strong reputation. Proverbs 20:6-7 (ESV): *"Many a man proclaims his own steadfast love, but a faithful man who can find? The righteous who walks in his integrity — blessed are his children after him."*

Speak clearly then let your actions follow through. Matthew 5:37 (ESV): *"Let what you say be simply 'Yes' or 'No'; anything more than this comes from evil."*

Lesson 6L: *Redeem* your mistakes

 Follow expert advice (*Redeem* your mistakes):

When a customer has a good reason to be unhappy, take extraordinary measures to correct your mistake. Often these will become your most loyal and outspoken customers. In some cases, your mistake was so bad that you need to give them a full refund. This hurts but is the right thing to do. The lost money won't matter for long, but your reputation lasts a lifetime. "Even when you don't think you did anything wrong, listen to customer criticism without getting defensive. See if there is any 'grain of truth' in what they are saying that you can use to make a positive change in your business" (Lee Murray).

Ask yourself (*Redeem* your mistakes):

Am I trying to make a quick sale or am I building long-term relationships?

_____

_____

What can I do to prevent repeating the same customer mistakes in the future?

_____

_____

 Meditate on these scriptures (*Redeem* your mistakes):

Going beyond what is expected to make restitution can reverse a bad impression. Luke 19:8 (ESV): *"And Zacchaeus stood and said to the Lord, 'Behold, Lord, the half of my goods I give to the poor. And if I have defrauded anyone of anything, I restore it fourfold."*

Lesson 6M: *Ask* for referrals

 Follow expert advice (*Ask* for referrals):

Customer love to both rant and rave about their purchases. Get on the right side of this tendency because people will trust the experience of your customers a lot more than your own marketing message! Ask these happy customers to spread the news and give you contact information of people they know who would be great customers. Don't forget to reach out to these potential customers and to thank the ones who referred them. A small gift would be appropriate to say thanks and to encourage them to do so again later. Since they already trust you, also ask friends, family and mentors to connect you to new customers.

 Ask yourself (*Ask* for referrals):

Who can I ask for referrals this week?

_____

_____

How can I build this into my regular interactions with my happy customers?

_____

_____

Where will I keep the contact information?

_____

_____

How can I remind myself to contact them to offer my products and services?

_____

_____

What is an inexpensive gift I can keep on hand to say thanks for referrals?

_____

_____

Meditate on these scriptures (*Ask* for referrals):

People are motivated to return a favor. Genesis 41:9-14 (NIV): "*Then the chief cupbearer said to Pharaoh, 'Today I am reminded of my shortcomings. Pharaoh was once angry with his servants, and he imprisoned me and the chief baker in the house of the captain of the guard. Each of us had a dream the same night, and each dream had a meaning of its own. Now a young Hebrew was there with us, a servant of the captain of the guard. We told him our dreams, and he interpreted them for us, giving each man the interpretation of his dream. And things turned out exactly as he interpreted them to us: I was restored to my position, and the other man was impaled.' So Pharaoh sent for Joseph, and he was quickly brought from the dungeon. When he had shaved and changed his clothes, he came before Pharaoh.*"

Lesson 6N: *Ask* for online reviews

 Follow expert advice (*Ask* for online reviews):

Every happy customer should be asked – and reminded only once if needed – to write a review for you on Google or other site used in your industry. Make a habit of this. It's not ethical to pay them to do this or to write a review yourself. If your diligence over time leads to top Google rankings and more five-star reviews than your competitors, people will believe you are trustworthy even before they meet you! This could become how you get most of your customers, and they may be willing to pay a higher price.

 ## *Ask* yourself (*Ask* for online reviews):

How can I build this practice into my routine with customers?

_____

_____

How many five-star reviews do I hope to earn by a year from today?

_____

_____

 ## *Meditate* on these scriptures (*Ask* for online reviews):

Trust is strengthened when others verify your trustworthiness. Deuteronomy 19:15 (NIV): *"One witness is not enough to convict anyone accused of any crime or offense they may have committed. A matter must be established by the testimony of two or three witnesses.*

Observe teens who follow advice:

After the kitchen was clean, Alejandro and Maria sat down together. Maria couldn't wait any longer, "Okay, okay, tell me what you heard. We need to fix this problem right away!"

Alejandro smiled. "For once, you're the excited one! I love it! Ok, we heard some bad news, but I think we can figure it out. The first is, some people said they were tired of trying to order from us, but not having success. Our food is good, but too hard to get. The initial excitement is gone. Second, we haven't changed our menu in a month. The students say they want some new choices. Third, we don't provide napkins like the other companies do. It is a small thing, but people expect it. So, let's talk this through and decide out how we can solve these problems."

 Avoid these top five mistakes:

1. Trying to sell to everyone rather than identifying and targeting your ideal customer.
2. Writing marketing messages that are more about you than about what you do for customers.
3. Not finding out where your ideal customers look for your product or service.
4. Letting fear or distractions keep you from frequently going

to see potential customers.

5. Building your whole business on only a few customers (true if losing your biggest client would be a major setback).

 Form these top five habits:

1. Truly listen and act on customer feedback.
2. Consistently provide a customer experience that is better than what they expect.
3. Ask all of your happy customers to write online reviews for you and to refer potential customers to you.
4. Invite your existing customers to buy more often and to buy your other products.
5. Track and steadily increase your monthly sales.

 Follow this real-life Honduran example:

Belinda Gonzalez is a gracious and encouraging woman who makes people feel very important. Even after being in business for 35 years, she sought out mentors to keep learning – even from people younger than her. That takes courage and humility. Listen in as she tells Odile Perez about her experience with customers.

Belinda with her Creating Jobs Inc mentors Carol & Larry McGehe

Belinda Gonzalez: *"At Eben-ezer, my construction supply company, we have seen many of our clients come and go. In fact, many of the clients we had in the beginning are no longer in business. This constant change has taught us the importance of continuously attracting new clients and effectively serving the current ones.*

We identified our ideal customers as engineers, architects, and medium-sized construction companies. One new strategy we're using to reach new customers is flooding engineering and architecture schools with publicity about our company. This informs engineers and architects on a national level about our services. We also offer free samples to potential customers so they can touch and feel the quality of our products. This has led to many new contracts.

We have created a detailed database to help us keep track of both potential and existing customers. We are constantly sending them personalized e-mails and updating our social media pages. We also send virtual cards on their birthdays, Christmas, and even Engineer Day and Architect Day! We like to go the extra mile to stay in touch.

Through the years, we have updated our marketing materials including our signs, business cards, flyers, and virtual catalogue. In our office we have a TV that continuously promotes our products. Our marketing channels include social media, personalized e-mails, onsite visits, construction fairs, and the Chamber of Construction magazine.

Recently, with a recommendation from Creating Jobs Inc, we restarted a practice that was fundamental to our growth in the first years of our business: making onsite visits to potential and current customers. As we began again, we were pleased with the excellent sales that came from it. Even though this takes lots of time and initiative, it has breathed new life into our company. We highly recommend it to you as it will keep your customer relationships fresh.

We also regularly ask our customers to refer us to others. We offer discounts to customers who give us referrals or promote our products on their social media pages.

Our sales are done via telephone marketing, social media, fairs, onsite visits, and in our office. Customers can pick up their purchase at our facility or we can deliver it to them. Our goal is to make the pick up or delivery process as convenient as possible for our customers.

We've learned that the best way to retain existing customers and acquire new ones is to give excellent service. We do this by keeping our promises, acknowledging our mistakes, and replacing damaged products at no cost. We visit construction sites that are using our products as a way to follow up and recommend the best ways to install our products. There is nothing better than a satisfied customer, who remains loyal and is willing to recommend us in their circle of influence. But we can't expect them to do all the work; we must keep searching for new customers while keeping our current ones happy. Never slack off as there's always a new way to reach new customers. So, always keep moving and innovating."

It is easy to get complacent after you attract a fair amount of customers. As you see with Belinda, the key is to keep or regain that get-customers-or-die sense of urgency you start off with. Notice the theme of persistent initiative in all of her efforts to attract and please her customers. She is a great example of trying lots of different approaches and consistently doing the things that work.

 Do with your group:

Carlos is starting a business to make signs and banners for small businesses in a large city. What places will his ideal customers look for his services? What marketing materials and marketing channels should he create to reach them? Re-read these expert advice sections: "Print your marketing materials" and "Build your marketing channels". Break into group of 3-4 for discussion then invite a few people to share their thoughts with the whole class.

Teacher's guide: Read them the questions first so they can listen to the expert advice with Carlos' situation in mind.

 Apply this module with:

PRAYER – Ask God for courage to go to visit my potential customers and ask them to buy. Pray for creativity as I write my marketing message.

RESEARCH – Find out who is most likely to buy my product and where they'd look for it.

CREATIVITY – Write five "headlines" and get feedback. Write the "body" of my marketing message.

ACTION – Go visit my ideal customers to establish relationships with them. Decide which types of marketing materials I need and work with a printer to produce them. Decide which online tools I need and work with suppliers to produce them.

CUSTOMERS – Write down description of my ideal customers. Make a list of 100 ideal customers. Ask my past customers to buy again and to buy other products I offer. Ask each customer over the next four weeks how their experience was buying from me and what I could do better, then make any needed changes. Ask happy customers for referrals and online reviews.

MENTORS – Ask about their experience in sales and customer service, especially how to handle it when I fail a customer.

MONEY – Track my monthly sales totals and make a goal to increase sales. Consider whether I am willing to lose money to save a relationship when I need to fix a problem with a customer.

TIME – Block out time to write my marketing message. Block out time to visit potential customers several times a week. Even after I make the sale, spend extra time with my customers to show that I care about them.

Practice values of Compassion International:

Integrity – Being reliable for your customers exhibits Christ-like character. Consistently providing the best solution pleases customers and makes you a more dependable person.

Excellence – When you do your best to serve customers, you find joy in bearing a faint reflection of God's perfection.

Stewardship – Finding who most needs your products is wise. Connecting your business to those it can best serve fulfills God's purpose for it.

Dignity – Since God is relational, so is the world He created. For this reason, the more personal your business interactions are, the more fulfilling they will be. So going to see your ideal customers in person honors their value as people.

Evaluate the teen business:

Pretend you are Mario, sitting in the kitchen when Alejandro and Maria ask you to come over and help solve these problems. What would be your suggestions? For each solution, explain:

- What your solution would look like.
- What it would cost to implement your solution.
- How your solution would be profitable for the business.

Then, ask a friend to evaluate your solutions as if they were Alejandro or Maria. From a business owner's perspective, what are the other factors that need to be considered when solving these problems? Be sure you both review the module so you don't miss anything!

Sum it up:

If you don't consistently make enough customers happy, you won't be in business long. "If your business was a solar system, your customers would be your sun – make sure everything revolves around them" (Lee Murray). So, put your best efforts into finding your ideal customers and providing an amazing solution. If you love your neighbors well, they will love you back! Customers talk, and a good reputation will be your biggest asset.

Use your *Start*Book Plan:

Now that you've completed this module, please fill out your *Start*Book Plan on the next page. Think about what you've learned and choose the most important goal for you to apply this module to your business over the next 12 months. Write down your goal, three actions to accomplish it, and dates to complete each one. Refer to your *Start*Book Plan often as a tool to grow your business.

StartBook Plan

6. Customers

Module snapshot: Identify your ideal customers and find the right message and means to reach them. Make them so happy that they bring their friends to you.

My #1 "Customers" goal for the next 12 months:

My top 3 action steps to accomplish this goal:

1.

Today's date: _____ Target completion date: _____ Actual completion date: _____

2.

Today's date: _____ Target completion date: _____ Actual complion date: _____

3.

Today's date: _____ Target completion date: _____ Actual completion date: _____

7. Growth

Module snapshot: Plan your next steps to put StartBook into practice. Decide whether you want to grow from a solopreneur into a CEO of a strong company.

Module 7: GROWTH

Consider module snapshot: Plan your next steps to put *Start*Book into practice. Decide whether you want to grow from a solopreneur into a CEO of a strong company.

Observe teens who need advice:

"Alejandro, I am so tired. I want to go to sleep – for a whole week," groaned Maria. "We are making four hundred tortillas a day. Cleaning up takes hours! And I still have to figure out a new menu for next week! Plus, our tomato supplier has been late three days in a row. I wonder if opening The Dream Tortilleria is becoming a nightmare!"

Alejandro felt exhausted too. He'd had to fire a delivery guy last week for stealing money. Taking on the extra deliveries had been good exercise, but he was getting worn out. When was he going to find a replacement? Plus, now that they were using the kitchen so much, his aunt had asked them to contribute to the cost of a new set of pots and pans! "Maria, you're right. I hardly have the energy to smile! We need to make some changes or we're going to collapse!"

Lesson 7A: *Review* and apply *Start*Book

 Follow expert advice (*Review* and apply *Start*Book):

Fill in your *Start*Book Big Picture (see table of contents) with single-sentence next steps for each point under: YOU, SOLUTION, PEOPLE, MONEY, LAUNCH & CUSTOMERS.

The *Start*Book Big Picture is like snorkeling in Roatan. It's a quick way to navigate the surface. But to get serious about exploring the coral reef, you need to go scuba diving which takes more time and effort. So please set aside *half a day*) to make detailed plans for each of the six steps using *Start*Book Plan (all seven Plans are compiled at the end of the book). This will give you the complete view of where you want to take your business.

To do so, look back through *Start*Book, especially at the notes you wrote in the "Ask yourself" sections. Decide which of these actions you'd like to complete over the coming 12 months. On a new computer document or in a notebook, write ten or more actions for each of the first six modules. When you're done, go back through them and select the most important three from each module. Write these on your *Start*Book Plan, then add the dates you plan to complete each goal. Put your completed *Start*Book Plan in a place you'll see them every day, and review your progress once a week as you plan the coming week – so you actually schedule your priorities

(Lesson 1G). Repeat this process once a year to update your plans. This amount of effort obviously requires a strong commitment. To motivate this, consider the fact that putting your business plan in writing makes your business twice as likely to succeed! (Small Biz Trends article: "A Business Plan Doubles Your Chances for Success", Jan 20, 2016 by Rieva Lesonsky

https://smallbiztrends.com/2010/06/business-plan-success-twice-as-likely.html)

Share your *Start*Book Big Picture and *Start*Book Plan with your mentors and parents, seeking their advice, accountability, and prayer for your new business.

 ***Ask* yourself (*Review* and apply *Start*Book):**

Looking at my completed *Start*Book Big Picture which of the six areas am I strongest and weakest in?

_____

_____

Which step will be my biggest focus in the next three months?

_____

_____

What is the biggest thing I've learned from *Start*Book?

_____

_____

When will I take half a day to set goals for the next 12 months using *Start*Book Plan?

_____

_____

After completing this, what did I learn from the process?

_____

_____

Whom will I seek feedback and accountability from?

_____

_____

Where will I put my *Start*Book Plan so I see it every day?

_____

_____

How will I remind myself to review it once a week and repeat the planning process once a year?

_____

_____

 Meditate on these scriptures (*Review* and apply *Start*Book):

Responsibility comes with your access to expert advice for starting a business. Luke 12:48 (NIV): *"But the one who does not know and does things deserving punishment will be beaten with few blows. From everyone who has been given much, much will be demanded; and from the one who has been entrusted with much, much more will be asked."*

God enables weak people to do great things. Hebrews 11:32-34 (NIV): *"And what more shall I say? I do not have time to tell about Gideon, Barak, Samson and Jephthah, about David and Samuel and the prophets, who through faith conquered kingdoms, administered justice, and gained what was promised; who shut the mouths of lions, quenched the fury of the flames, and escaped the edge of the sword; whose weakness was turned to strength; and who became powerful in battle and routed foreign armies."*

God empowers your faith-filled actions. 2 Thessalonians 1:11 (NIV): *"With this in mind, we constantly pray for you, that our God may make you worthy of his calling, and that by his power he may* *bring to fruition your every desire for goodness and your every deed prompted by faith."*

Good planning and hard work lead to prosperity, but hasty shortcuts lead to poverty. Proverbs 21:5 (NIV): *"The plans of the diligent lead to profit as surely as haste leads to poverty."*

Submitting your plans to God in prayer is wise. James 4:13-15 (NIV): *"Come now, you who say, "Today or tomorrow we will go into such and such a town and spend a year there and trade and make a profit"— yet you do not know what tomorrow will bring. What is your life? For you are a mist that appears for a little time and then vanishes. Instead you ought to say, "If the Lord wills, we will live and do this or that."*

Following through on your plans is what counts. Proverbs 14:23 (NIV): *"All hard work brings a profit, but mere talk leads only to poverty.*

Lesson 7B: *Commit* to grow

 Follow expert advice (*Commit* to grow):

Healthy things grow, so your business should be steadily growing as well. If you're not moving forward, your competitors will find ways to win over your customers. Healthy growth can be fast or slow, it can be in size or excellence.

Discern which of these are the best ways to grow the *size* of your business: expanding the geographic reach of your business, selling to more customers within your current territory, or selling additional types of products and services to your existing customers.

Discern which of these are the best ways to grow the *excellence* of your business: your own growth in character, continuous product improvement, better relationships with employees and suppliers, new and better systems, better marketing messages and materials, employees growing in skills and leadership and teamwork, less debt, more savings, better equipment, less waste, and higher customer satisfaction.

 Ask yourself (*Commit* to grow):

Am I committed to growth or am I complacent?

_____

_____

How will I grow the *size* of my business?

_____

_____

How will I grow the *excellence* of my business?

 Meditate on these scriptures (*Commit to grow*):

Always press forward. Philippians 3:13-14 (NIV): *"Brothers and sisters, I do not consider myself yet to have taken hold of it. But one thing I do: Forgetting what is behind and straining toward what is ahead, I press on toward the goal to win the prize for which God has called me heavenward in Christ Jesus."*

Growing in excellence pleases God. Colossians 3:23 (ESV): *"Whatever you do, work at it with all your heart, as working for the Lord, not for human masters."*

Multiplying what God entrusted to you brings joy and reward. Matthew 25:20-21 (NIV): *"The man who had received five bags of gold brought the other five. 'Master,' he said, 'you entrusted me with five bags of gold. See, I have gained five more.' 'His master replied, 'Well done, good and faithful servant! You have been faithful with a few things; I will put you in charge of many things. Come and share your master's happiness!'"*

Lesson 7C: *Keep* learning using GrowBook

 Follow expert advice (*Keep* learning using *Grow*Book):

After you launch your business and begin to apply much of this book, begin to read *Grow*Book which we wrote to help you grow your startup into a mature business. Creating Jobs Inc designed *Grow*Book to be used after *Start*Book. It will help you transition from being a technician who can make a product to a CEO who develops employees into strong leaders and entrusts them to run much of the operations, freeing you to focus on innovation and strategy. It is the difference between working "in" your business and working "on" your business.

Now that you've established a working business, *Grow*Book will help you take a step back to discern what the true vision, mission, and values of your company should be. This would be a worthless exercise if you didn't actually use them. But remember, you're co-creating the future here! These foundational documents can get you and your employees all working in the same direction to make something amazing. Vision, mission, and values should be used to shape long term goals, short term goals, who you hire, and the way you work every day.

*Grow*Book also goes into a lot more detail on how to develop systems, drive innovation, manufacture your products, refine your branding, and grow your sales. With your employees, GrowBook will help you develop: leaders, teamwork, and teammates who care about your company. Regarding money, GrowBook goes deeper into cash flow, savings strategy, negotiating good deals, using financial statements, and resisting corruption. An entire module on giving back explores how to mentor other entrepreneurs and serve with your time, talent, and treasure. You can use *Grow*Book on your own with a group of other entrepreneurs. Read and apply lots of other books and articles on business. As we discussed in Lesson 1C, these ingredients will lead to new ingenious new recipes you've yet to create!

 Ask yourself (*Keep* learning using *Grow*Book):

Do I want to create only a job for myself or a company where many will thrive?

_____

_____

Am I willing to train and trust employees to produce my product so I can focus on building my business?

_____

_____

Am I ready to develop foundational documents, learn to use financial statements, develop stronger systems, and use business to serve my community?

_____

_____

If my answer is "yes", when will I begin reading *Grow*Book?

_____

_____

Will I work through it with other entrepreneurs?

_____

_____

 Meditate **on these scriptures (*Keep* learning using *Grow*Book):**

Wise leaders seek out others to learn from. Proverbs 24:5-6 (NIV): *"The wise prevail through great power, and those who have knowledge muster their strength. Surely you need guidance to wage war, and victory is won through many advisers."*

Jesus is your example of continuous learning. Luke 2:52 (NIV): *"And Jesus grew in wisdom and stature, and in favor with God and man."*

 Observe teens who follow advice:

The next morning, when they walked into the kitchen, Maria was beaming. "Ok Alejandro, I have some ideas. I stayed up last night praying, reading my Bible, and reviewing our business books. I have new energy – but we need to make some big changes."

Alejandro couldn't agree more. "Maria, you're right. I've been praying too, asking God to show us what to do. I'm still tired, but your happy smile is enough. Let's figure it out."

Maria laughed. "Hey, we can do it. But there's a lot to do! First, we need to raise our prices again. That way we can hire an assistant cook and better delivery guys. It cost us a lot of money to have that guy steal from us. And I need help in the kitchen before I collapse. Also, we need to save more – so one day, we can open a store right next to the university. Then we won't have these long delivery times. Our food will be fresher, hotter, better! Third, we need to set some goals. If we keep growing without a plan, we're always going to be worn out."

Getting excited, Alejandro exclaimed, "Those are great ideas! Look, if I can hire someone to make my deliveries, I can start negotiating some better deals for us. If we get the right person for the job, I know they'll even help us sell more tortillas. And I think I know a great person to help you cook – she's got lots of creative ideas too! We definitely need a new tomato supplier. Plus, I need to find some new pots and pans for my aunt. And a better deal on our posters. Then our biggest need: a good store at a great price in just the right location! Let's pray together – and then start writing this down!"

 Avoid these top five mistakes:

1. Letting urgent things crowd out the important discipline of setting goals.
2. Not prioritizing your goals.
3. Not breaking big goals down into small steps with target completion dates.
4. Forgetting to implement your goals.
5. Getting bored after your business is established rather than finding joy in making it better every day.

 Form these top five habits:

1. Take half a day to update your *Start*Book Plan once a year.
2. Post your *Start*Book Plan where you will see it daily.
3. Review your progress once a week and schedule your action items for the upcoming week.
4. Always have in mind how you plan to grow your business in both size and excellence.
5. Read and apply one module of *Grow*Book every month.

Follow this real-life Honduran example:

At the age of three, a little girl who lived in a dangerous neighborhood was sponsored through Compassion International. Her name is Joyce. When she was 12 years old, she started learning to cut hair and do nails at her church's Compassion program. That is exactly the kind of opportunity she needed, and guess what she did next? Since jobs are rare in her neighborhood, Joyce started her own salon there! She committed herself to learning the difficult task of running a business effectively. Even as a young teenager, she worked diligently making her business better and bigger over a period of five years. The result is that she now has three employees, serves 80 customers a week, and continues to grow her business!

Joyce with her mentor

Joyce's customers come from near and far because of her excellent work and the welcoming environment she has created (which includes sharing encouragement, a complimentary drink and a snack). Customers share their problems with her and even older women ask for her advice. She is living out her faith by providing an excellent service along with tender compassion. It took years of making goals and following through on them while trusting God to bring the results.

Her heart to serve even extends beyond her business. How does she find time to teach youth in her community how to cut hair and be the primary caregiver for her three younger brothers? Since her mother is out of the country, Joyce is like a mom to them and reads the bible to them every evening. Even though she is only 17 years old, guess how many people she supports in her household? Eight! And she pays the rent. Wow!

Joyce could keep all of her business profits for her own desires, but her desire is to glorify the Lord so she faithfully gives 10% to support the ministry of her church family. All of these good decisions have matured Joyce beyond her years. Even with all she's accomplished, Joyce knows that her hard work was empowered by God's grace and supported by her church's Compassion mentors. Her large brown eyes still sparkle with the playfulness of youth, but also with the confident maturity of someone who is being powerfully used by God in her family, church and community.

Like this module advises, Joyce sets goals and works to achieve them. She currently is working with her mentors on a plan to attract enough new customers to afford a larger building for her salon. She's committed to growing her business and growing as a leader. One of the ways she keeps investing in herself is by taking university classes in the evenings. Joyce knows it is important to be hungry to learn. Joyce is eagerly reading GrowBook and applying it to her business. She's a lot like the servant in Jesus' parable who received talents from God and wisely multiplied them tenfold. We pray that you'll follow her great example.

 ## *Do* with your group:

Joyce is busy cutting and styling her customers' hair, going to college at night, and looking after her young brothers. How will she find time to think about the direction of her business and set goals for the year? Break into pairs to brainstorm solutions for Joyce then share them with the whole class.

Teacher's note: You may want to refer back to the expert advice section of Lesson 1G on page 47 (Make time work for you).

 ## *Apply* this module with:

PRAYER – Seek God's wisdom and direction in making plans for growth. While it may be hard to imagine beyond next month, ask God to help me envision my business in three years.

RESEARCH – Gather facts to help me decide which of these three strategies is my best growth opportunity: selling new products to my existing customers, finding more customers in my existing territory, or expanding my territory.

CREATIVITY – Fill out my *StartBook* Big Picture. Fill out my

*Start*Book Plan. Decide how to grow the size and excellence of my business.

ACTION – Get a copy of *Grow*Book and read it.

CUSTOMERS – Ask them what new solutions they might want from my business.

MENTORS – Ask for accountability and guidance to develop habits that remind me to act on my plans. Ask a mentor to help me apply a module per month of *Grow*Book.

MONEY – Set savings goals for equipment and emergencies.

TIME – Block out a half-day to fill out my *Start*Book Plan.

Practice values of Compassion International:

Integrity – Following through on goals you've set demonstrates integrity to your employees. They'll trust your leadership more and stay with you – *especially* if you've set goals that will benefit them.

Excellence – Never becoming complacent with the success of your business reveals a pursuit of greatness that reflects our great God. Constantly learning and improving your business is the best way to stay focused.

Stewardship – Reviewing and applying what you've learned through *Start*Book is an important way to steward what God has invested in you. As the Bible says: "From everyone who has been given much, much will be demanded; and from the one who has been entrusted with much, much more will be asked" (Luke 12:48

NIV). Not putting what you've learned into action would be a colossal waste of what's been entrusted to you.

Dignity – Planning is an awesome way to co-create the future alongside God! "Many are the plans in a person's heart, but it is the LORD's purpose that prevails" (Proverbs 19:21 NIV). While you don't know what future God has in store, He allows you to shape it through you decisions and actions. How amazing is that? So, approach goal-setting as an awesome privilege, a mysterious partnership with the Almighty who reveals who you are as a royal son or daughter.

Evaluate the teen business:

Imagine that you are a local business leader at Alejandro and Maria's church. Noticing how tired they look one Sunday, you invite them to your home for a meal. As they share the problems of their growing business with you, how would you respond?

- How would you encourage their hearts?
- What questions would you ask?
- What resources could you share?
- What advice would you give in an uplifting way?
- Who could you introduce them to for additional advice or help?
- How would you pray for them?

Sum it up:

Planning is never urgent but always important. While it's hard to find time to set goals, it is invigorating to look into the future and shape it with God's help! So, invest the time and follow through on your goals. You'll be amazed at the results. Use *Grow*Book to grow your business in size and excellence. Be strong in the Lord!

Use your *Start*Book Plan:

Now that you've completed this module, please fill out your *Start*Book Plan on the next page. Think about what you've learned and choose the most important goal for you to apply this module to your business over the next 12 months. Write down your goal, three actions to accomplish it, and dates to complete each one. Refer to your *Start*Book Plan often as a tool to grow your business.

Thanks for reading and applying StartBook. We pray that your business will bring you much joy as you co-create alongside the Almighty! Never tire of getting better every day or finding new ways to use your products, services, time, money, jobs and influence to bless your community and world!

StartBook Plan

1. Growth

Module snapshot: Plan your next steps to put StartBook into practice. Decide whether you want to grow from a solopreneur into a CEO of a strong company.

My #1 "Growth" goal for the next 12 months:

My top 3 action steps to accomplish this goal:

1.

Today's date: _____ Target completion date: _____ Actual completion date: _____

2.

Today's date: _____ Target completion date: _____ Actual compl 'ion date: _____

3.

Today's date: _____ Target completion date: _____ Actual completion date: _____

*Start*Book

Snapshot:

Mobilize your strengths, resources and teammates to bring an innovative solution to customers who want it.

StartBook

At-a-Glance

Mobilize your strengths, resources and teammates to bring an innovative solution to customers who want it.

1. You

Learn what makes a mature entrepreneur. Assess yourself and plan to grow.

2. Solution

Create a unique solution to a real problem, letting your customers' input shape your product or service. Build your business identity around that solution and design systems to produce your product efficiently and safely.

3. People

Appreciate and learn from these groups of people who are vital to your success. Build trusting win-win relationships with them.

4. Money

There's never enough money for everything, so you must direct it toward your priorities. Diligently follow these best practices to control your money and patiently build wealth.

5. Launch

Give attention to these important details to plan a successful launch.

6. Customers

Identify your ideal customers and find the right message and means to reach them. Make them so happy that they bring their friends to you.

7. Growth

Plan your next steps to put StartBook into practice. Decide whether you want to grow from a solopreneur into a CEO of a strong company.

What does each aspect of your business need?

Write "maintain", "fine-tune", or "overhaul" under each icon.

My *BiG* Focus:

My top goal to
move it forward:

StartBook Plan

Module snapshot: Learn what makes a mature entrepreneur. Assess yourself and plan to grow.

My #1 "You" goal for the next 12 months:

My top 3 action steps to accomplish this goal:

1.

Today's date: _____ Target completion date: _____ Actual completion date: _____

2.

Today's date: _____ Target completion date: _____ Actual completion date: _____

3.

Today's date: _____ Target completion date: _____ Actual completion date: _____

StartBook Plan

2. Solution

Module snapshot: Create a unique solution to a real problem, letting your customers' input shape your product or service. Build your business identity around that solution and design systems to produce your product efficiently and safely.

My #1 "Solution" goal for the next 12 months:

My top 3 action steps to accomplish this goal:

1.

Today's date: _____ Target completion date: _____ Actual completion date: _____

2.

Today's date: _____ Target completion date: _____ Actual completion date: _____

3.

Today's date: _____ Target completion date: _____ Actual completion date: _____

*Start*Book Plan

3. People

Module snapshot: Appreciate and learn from these groups of people who are vital to your success. Build trusting win-win relationships with them.

My #1 "People" goal for the next 12 months:

[   ]

My top 3 action steps to accomplish this goal:

1.

Today's date: _____ Target completion date: _____ Actual completion date: _____

2.

Today's date: _____ Target completion date: _____ Actual compl ⁀ion date: _____

3.

Today's date: _____ Target completion date: _____ Actual completion date: _____

StartBook Plan

4. Money

Module snapshot: There's never enough money for everything, so you must direct it toward your priorities. Diligently follow these best practices to control your money and patiently build wealth.

My #1 "Money" goal for the next 12 months:

My top 3 action steps to accomplish this goal:

1.

Today's date: _____ Target completion date: _____ Actual completion date: _____

2.

Today's date: _____ Target completion date: _____ Actual compl \ion date: _____

3.

Today's date: _____ Target completion date: _____ Actual completion date: _____

*Start*Book Plan

5. Launch

Module snapshot: Give attention to these important details to plan a successful launch.

My #1 "Launch" goal for the next 12 months:

My top 3 action steps to accomplish this goal:

1.

Today's date: _____ Target completion date: _____ Actual completion date: _____

2.

Today's date: _____ Target completion date: _____ Actual completion date: _____

3.

Today's date: _____ Target completion date: _____ Actual completion date: _____

StartBook Plan

6. Customers

Module snapshot: Identify your ideal customers and find the right message and means to reach them. Make them so happy that they bring their friends to you.

My #1 "Customers" goal for the next 12 months:

My top 3 action steps to accomplish this goal:

1.

Today's date: _____ Target completion date: _____ Actual completion date: _____

2.

Today's date: _____ Target completion date: _____ Actual compl ٰ ion date: _____

3.

Today's date: _____ Target completion date: _____ Actual completion date: _____

*Start*Book Plan

1. Growth

Module snapshot: Plan your next steps to put StartBook into practice. Decide whether you want to grow from a solopreneur into a CEO of a strong company.

My #1 "Growth" goal for the next 12 months:

My top 3 action steps to accomplish this goal:

1.

Today's date: _____ Target completion date: _____ Actual completion date: _____

2.

Today's date: _____ Target completion date: _____ Actual compl Yon date: _____

3.

Today's date: _____ Target completion date: _____ Actual completion date: _____

Contributors

Evan Keller, Lead Author & General Editor – Evan is married to his beloved wife Karen of 25 years – a former nurse who's an awesome cook and baker. In addition to escaping to the mountains, they enjoy their life together in Central Florida, which is near to their super-fun 13 nieces and nephews! Evan is addicted to playing basketball, and dabbles in off-road biking, paddling, and mountain backpacking. He appreciates close friends, crossing cultures, art, blues music, and books on theology and business. At work, he's the Founder/Executive Director of Creating Jobs Inc & Founder/CEO of Tree Work Now Inc.

Odile Perez, Author & Translator – Odile wrote four of the *Start*Book case studies and translated it into Spanish. She cares for her mom along with her stepdad in Orlando, FL, has lived in six countries, and is native to the Dominican Republic. She currently works as an administrative assistant and translator at Creating Jobs Inc. and Tree Work Now Inc. She is an independent sales consultant for Organo. A highlight from her past experiences was serving as a Learning and Advocacy Advisor in the Diaspora Volunteering Program of Voluntary Service Overseas (VSO) in the UK.

Carson Weitnauer, Author – Carson wrote the fictional narratives of the teen-owned tortilleria and came up with the name "*Start*Book". He also co-wrote the small group curriculum *Everyday Questions* and co-edited the book *True Reason*. Carson graduated from Rhodes College (Memphis, TN) with a BA in philosophy and from Gordon-Conwell Theological Seminary with an M.Div. Carson serves as chairman of the board of Creating Jobs Inc, the business development non-profit which published *Start*Book. He lives in Atlanta, GA with his wife and two children.

Jeff Hostetter, Author – Jeff wrote one of the case studies, has several quotes in *Start*Book, and is further contextualizing its 57 lessons for use by Compassion International. He has been happily married to Diane for 27 years! They live in Lancaster, PA with their children Adam (21) and Kelly (14). Jeff enjoys riding his electric skateboard, serves as a small group leader to his church family, has a deep relationship with Compassion International, and is a lead mentor with Creating Jobs Inc in Honduras. He is Co-founder and former CEO of Elexio church software, current Co-owner (with his son Adam) of Fresh Healthy Vending. He is Founder of Kingdom Impact and Chapter President of Christian Business Fellowship.

Carol McGehe, International Mentor – Carol serves with Creating Jobs Inc in Honduras, where she wrote two of the case studies about entrepreneurs she mentors along with her husband and lead mentor, Larry McGehe. She is retired from a career as a curriculum specialist.

Lee Murray, Marketing Expert – Lee provided several quotes throughout *Start*Book. His experience comes as the principal at Signal Media, as a former lead mentor and current board member at Creating Jobs Inc.

Dr. Carol Keller-Vlangas, Bibliography Creator & Proof-reader – Carol utilized her experience as an English teacher and career educator who has invested in thousands of teens over the years, including her son Evan!

Mulyo Candra Amerta, Illustrator – Mulyo took the photograph of a pine cone from my neighbor's tree and made the splendid wpap illustration seen on the front cover, title page, and *Start*Book Snapshot! Mulyo lives in Kudus, Indonesia and you can hire him on fivver.com as "amertacan".

Pinki Gupta, Formatter – Pinki did a splendid job of adding all the icons, photos, diagrams, and page numbers into the manuscript. She provided a clean manuscript to take to print. Pinki lives in India and you can hire her for your formatting projects on Fivver.com where she goes by "pinkszzz".

 **Compassion International Honduras** – One of our *Start*Book authors, Jeff Hostetter, has developed a deep bond with Compassion through decades of sponsoring Honduran children, visiting them, and motivating scores of employees and friends to do the same. Our partnership with Compassion has been a joy as both parties sense that God has brought us together to do something beautiful that neither could do alone. They have a vision to empower some of their 50,000 sponsored teens to create their own opportunities through entrepreneurship using *Start*Book and lessons developed from it.

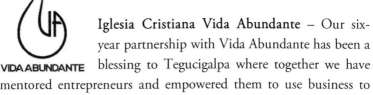 **Iglesia Cristiana Vida Abundante** – Our six-year partnership with Vida Abundante has been a blessing to Tegucigalpa where together we have mentored entrepreneurs and empowered them to use business to serve. Their ministry to entrepreneurs, "Global Empresarios en Pacto", is full of strong leaders who have become dear friends and ministry partners. We cherish these brothers and sisters in Christ!

Case Study Contributors – Maria Villela, Suyapa Parafita, Saúl Contreras, Hector Euceda, Joyce (last name omitted to protect privacy of this youth entrepreneur), Fausto Varelo, and Belinda Gonzalez. Each of these runs a successful business in Honduras that *Start*Book uses to illustrate the advice of a particular module. We appreciate the time they took to share their stories, which are an inspiration to us all!

Colibri Translation Services, John Adams – Translator (French, Haitian Creole), colibritranslation@gmail.com.

 **Tree Work Now Inc** - A big thanks to my brother and business partner, Dani Keller, and our great team at Tree Work Now Inc. By skillfully filling some of the roles I used to fill, they empower the work of Creating Jobs Inc – including this book.

 **Creating Jobs Inc** – Its board members, fellow mentors, and inspiring entrepreneurs are weaved into the fabric of this book. Thank you all!

Bibliography

Brodsky, N., & Burlingham, B. (2008). *Street Smarts*. New York: Portfolio Hardcover.

Buffett, W. (2013, May 1). *The Buffett Formula: How to get Smarter*. Retrieved December 27, 2017, from Farnam Street Blog: https://www.farnamstreetblog.com/2013/05/the-buffett-formula-how-to-get-smarter/

Collins, J. (2011). *Good to Great*. New York: Harper Collins.

Covey, S. (1989). *The Seven Habits of Highly Effective People*. New York: Simon and Schuster.

DenBesten, K. (2008). *Shine*. Shippensburg: Destiny Image.

Elwell, E. (2017, November 25). *Co.Starter: Core Program Participant Binder*. Chattanooga: The Company Lab.

Gladwell, M. (2008). *Outliers: The Story of Success*. New York: Little Brown and Company.

Griffith, E. (2016, September 25). *Why Startups Fail, According to their Founders*. Retrieved December 20, 2017, from Fortune Magazine:http://fortune.com/2014/09/25/why-startups-fail-according-to-their-founders.html

Heath, C., & Heath, D. (2008). *Made to Stick*. New York: Random House.

Holy Bible. (n.d.). King James Version.

Hood, J. (2013). *Imitating God in Christ*. Downers Grove: Intervarsity Press.

Kahle, D. (2016). Model or Leaders Staff Pick. *The Good Book on Business.* Houston: Center for Christianity in Business.

Keller, E. (2015). *GrowBook: 25 Essential Drivers of Small Business Success in the Developing World.* DeLand: Creating Jobs Inc

Lesonsky, R. (2016, January 20). *A Business Plan Doubles Your Chances for Success.* Retrieved December 21, 2017, from Small Business Trends:https://smallbiztrends.com/2010/06/business-plann-success-twice-as-likely.html

Medina, J. (2014). *Brain Rules.* Seattle: Pear Press.

Murray, L. (2017, November 5). E. Keller, Interviewer.

Panasiuk, A. (2015). *Decisiones Que Cuentan.* Nashville: Grupo Nelson.

Partners Worldwide. (2014). Business Curriculum for Small and Medium Enterprises. *Partners Worldwide Business Curriculum for Small and Medium Enterprises.* Grand Rapids: Partners Worldwide.

Robinson, J. (2013, May). *Entrepreneur Magazine,* p. 64.

Rohn, J. (2016, February 27). *Personal Quotation by Fausto Varelo.* Retrieved December 20, 2017, from John Rohn Personal Development Seminar:https://youtube/jnBdNkkceZw

Steiner, A. (2017, September 15). What's in Your Hands? (E. Keller, Interviewer)

Witherington, B. (2011). *Work.* Grand Rapids: Eerdmans.

Tzu, S. (2017). *The Art of War.* London: MacMillan Collector's Library.

Made in the USA
Columbia, SC
04 February 2019